PUBLISHED BY
ETERNAL PRESENCE
San Francisco, CA

MATTHEW & TERCES
ENGELHART

KINDRED SPIRIT

FULFILLING
LOVE'S PROMISE

Art Direction &

JON MARRO

Graphic Design

Kindred Spirit:
Fulfilling Love's Promise
By: Matthew and Terces Engelhart

Printed in China by:
Robert M. Clark, CEO
www.resourcelogicinc.com
Printed on Recycled paper using Vegetable- Based Ink

ISBN: 978-1-4507-3918-4

Published by:
Eternal Presence
P.O. Box 10131
Oakland, CA 94610
www.cafegratitude.com

Art Direction and Design by:
Jon Marro
www.jonmarro.com

Lovingly Edited by: Tina Rieman

Photos of Authors by:
Richard Gillette (page 80)
Rory Finney (page108)

YOU ARE

LOVED

Only the heart can hold a paradox,
the mind is too linear; life is a paradox.
—Adama

I Am a Kindred Spirit

While working on this book, Terces had the insight to write it in the first person. This "first person" presentation makes the entire book an affirmation of your life. So, now you can say to yourself, "I will be reading this as my story, my transformation, and my insights. I am empowered and excited to open myself up to the possibility of being a Kindred Spirit in my life, right now. I can't wait to experience how I feel, what I learn, and the breakthroughs I will have. I am so thrilled to be experiencing relationship in a new way, ushering in a new view of partnership and community. I am grateful for this opportunity."

Whenever there is a personal story from either Matthew's life (blue) or Terces' life (red), those appear in the colored ink indicated. When there is a story from anyone else's life, I will say so. These personal stories add new perspectives and additional opportunities for me to see myself in what is being shared. Thank you to all who shared so deeply with me in this process.

The ground submits to the sky and suffers whatever comes. Tell me, is the Earth worse for giving in like that?
—Rumi

It Is Never Too Late
How I keep my heart open is I don't let it close.
-Terces Engelhart

Looking at my life, one might wonder why anyone would listen to me when it comes to relationship. I have been married four times for a total of twenty-four years. From one perspective, I have failed many times; from another, I succeeded many times because I didn't give up. What I can tell you is that relationship is the most important aspect of my life. My relationship with God, my relationship with my children and their families, my relationship with my community, my relationship with my husband and my relationship with myself.

When I was a child all I ever wanted was to grow up, fall in love with a man, get married and have children. I was raised in a very traditional middle-class American home. My mother was passionate about being a full time housewife and mom. I am the youngest of three girls. My father was a U.S. Navy pilot who retired after nearly thirty years of active duty. He then became a high school mathematics teacher for another twenty-five years. My parents were married almost fifty years when my father passed away. My mother lived another sixteen years and missed him every day.

Although my mother and father deeply loved one another, I wouldn't say that I learned a lot from them about creating and sus

HOW I KEEP MY HEART OPEN
is

I DON'T LET IT CLOSE.

taining a healthy relationship, other than the importance of doing what pleases someone else, even if it is to the detriment of my own well-being. I was actually taught never to say "no," particularly to someone older or in a position of authority. That lesson led to my being sexually abused by the time I was sixteen years old - and then keeping the abuse a secret for twenty years, while I suffered with an eating disorder and lived a lie.

I was married when I was nineteen. He was my high school sweetheart. We were divorced a year later. Five years after that, I married a Viet Nam veteran who returned to the U.S. addicted to heroin. After five years of marriage with him, and with one son and pregnant with our daughter, I left the marriage when he became physically abusive. After another five years had elapsed, I married the bartender who hired me when I'd left my husband. We were married for twelve years and had a son together. During our marriage he joined the Navy. While he was deployed overseas I went into recovery. I began to tell the truth about the abuse I had endured and the lies about my past. It was pretty messy, and although we tried our best to keep our marriage together, I was too young and immature in my recovery, and we were divorced approximately a year later. For the next 15 years I was a single mother. I felt defeated in my ability to sustain an intimate partnership. Although everything I knew hadn't worked, I did not give up. Instead, I reached a special destination, the place of "not knowing," of "letting go." I was open to discovering something new and surrendering to the unknown.

When I met Matthew, I was 50 years old and starting to think that perhaps the relationship I dreamed of was going to happen in another lifetime. He and I became the best of friends. One day he said to me, "I would like to have a more committed romantic relationship with you."

I laughed in reply, saying, "You're not my type!"

He responded, "What do you mean I'm not your type? We're best friends!" From that day until now we have been together nearly every day. We have the relationship I always dreamed of having. We're still best friends, lovers, parents, grandparents, partners in business and community leaders.

So here's why you might listen to me: I've come through the challenges of relationship. I practice what we share with you in this book. I continue to be empowered and in love with my husband, effective in leadership and fulfilled in all the other relationships that define my life.

Most importantly, I'm living by example. With my personal history, if I can create great relationships, so can you!

꧁꧁꧁꧁꧁꧁꧁꧁꧁꧁꧁꧁꧁꧁꧁꧁꧁꧁꧁꧁꧁꧁꧁

Since forever we've argued about, killed each other over, and built
our identities around the best way, the "right way" to love God.
As if God needs our love served on a special platter or we need to
love God correctly to get front row seats.
How absurd.
God is love, the consciousness of Oneness.
How can there be a right way to love?
Love is the state of unconditional inclusion.
Our opinions are the obstacles.
Love occupies the empty,
but even God cannot fill what is already full.
The chaos of love is too much to hold,
so we sell out for the refuge of rightness.
But judgment and surrender do not serve the same master.

-Matthew Engelhart

꧁꧁꧁꧁꧁꧁꧁꧁꧁꧁꧁꧁꧁꧁꧁꧁꧁꧁꧁꧁꧁꧁꧁

*There are hundreds of ways to kneel
and kiss the ground.*
—Rumi

I Am Community
Am I willing to share it all?

When Rudi Giuliani mocked Barack Obama at the 2008 Republican convention for being a "community builder" I was at first appalled, but now, I see it as a clear sign of a changing of the guard: the myth of the lone gunslinger sleeping solo under the frontier sky is being usurped by a welcoming community gathered around a long harvest table.

When I was seven years old, a couple who had been friends and neighbors of my family were killed in an automobile accident. My parents took their five orphaned children and had them come to live with us as our new brothers and sisters. I had been the youngest child, but now I had a three-year-old sister. This heroic act by my mother and father, and the ensuing training I received in sharing space, are formative events in the development of my capacity as a community-builder, even though I confess that I have resisted this vocation. Many times I have pursued the Horatio Alger fable of individual responsibility. It has had great value. But now, inspired by the necessity of community, my focus is on birthing our collective awakening to unconditional love.

Kindred Spirit is a guide to communion in all relationships. In these pages you'll find the tools I wield to harmonize and presence [that is, be the embodiment of] unconditional love with two hundred employees, my wife, my ex-wife, five children, four grandchildren, landlords, tenants, two farms, our community in Mexico, all my friends, and even telemarketers. All my relations! My authority is in the practice as well as in my unwillingness to sell out on love's presence. Facing evidence to the contrary in today's headlines (there are atrocities happening in the Congo and Gaza as I write), I continue to have an overwhelming faith in a great awakening emerging for us all.

My date of birth, June 12th, is called "the day of buoyant optimism." I'll carry that flag for all my days.

WHAT WOUNDS ARE MY RELATIONSHIPS REVEALING TO ME?

you don't have to go looking for love when it's where you come from.
—Werner Erhard

BEING A KINDRED SPIRIT
"What wounds are my relationships revealing to me?"

Relationship is a healing path, an access to recover from the illusion of separation, to awaken from the split. Using the mirror of relationship is a path, like that of the ascetic, the householder, the healer, the ecstatic; it has its particular qualities, challenges and surrender opportunities. I say that some degree of mastery in relationship is essential for living an inspired life – for making a difference. This of course is not the Truth; it's just my created context for relationship and the one I am sharing with you now.

I am already unconditional love. Oneness is my authentic self. My mission as a prodigal son or daughter is to bring awareness about the lie of separation and to yield to an ever-expanding presence of love that will occupy me to the degree that my ego can get out of the way. Relationships of any kind (intimate, employee-employer, family, teacher-student, etc.) are training opportunities – revealing tools to uncover how my egoic machinery is worshiping fear and denying me my divine inheritance, which is Love. While occupation by the Supreme-Love-Presence might be sufficient enough to contemplate the conscious use of relationship as an awakening tool, there are other, more timely considerations. I could assert that the world is in a relationship crisis, that the "unworkability" of humanity is a function of the defensiveness of the ego and its insatiable desires that emanate from its illusion of isolation. How much of my resources and time are spent in securing my position, my country (defense budgets), my stuff, my house, my success (competitiveness)? How often do I find myself trying to

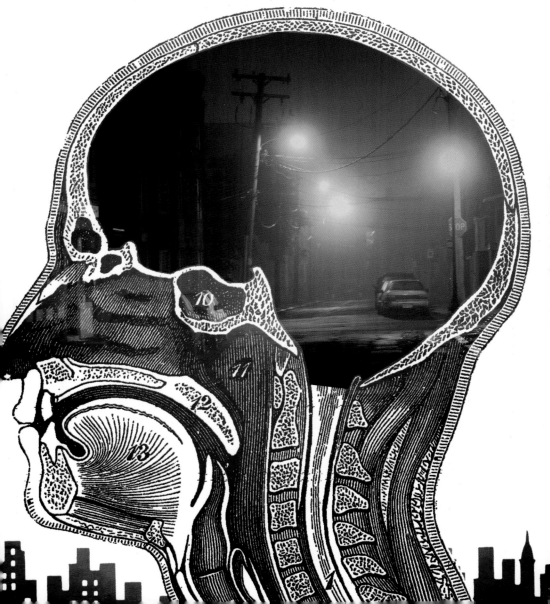

feed my "hungry ghost," get love from others and get fulfillment from things? All human communication can be distilled to two assertions: either "I want love," or "I am love." The first statement places love outside of me and creates love as something to possess. The second assertion, however, is an internal experience shaped by my awareness whereby love is experienced as a presence, a reality waiting to inhabit my consciousness.

I am considering that the monologue in my head is like a bad neighborhood, and it is better not to go in there alone. In a Kindred Spirit relationship, an intention of awakening is agreed upon, the safe container of acceptance is created, and a partnership of mutual discovery and of holding space (a compassionate witnessing space) for one another is experienced.

We all want to take care of each other, but sometimes we're too afraid to step up and do it. Community is the only way out of the current storm enveloping the world. This rescue will require a cavalry of people willing to commit to and use relationship as a path of liberation. This liberation will fulfill our awakening, while leaving "classroom earth" in good shape for future generations of sentient beings. Shifting to the identification of myself as a space of love and a being of service, attending to the whole, rather than a needy identity, is the merry game that's afoot. Relationship is a means to reveal my ego's authority and invite it to stand down. This is regime change. Love is calling me home.

Carpenters bend wood, fletchers straighten arrows, wise men fashion themselves.
—Buddha

It is all Being
*Can I see that whatever experience I am having,
I am the one creating it?*

What if life is all being? Looking at my experience of life, not necessarily believing what anyone else says about it, what do I see? What is creating my experience? Is my experience of my life based on my actual circumstances, or is it based on what I'm *thinking, saying, doing* and *believing,* and on my *attitude* about my circumstances? How am I distinguishing "my being?" How do I experience life as a *three dimensional* being on this planet? The human "being" part of me thinks, talks, believes, does, and has an attitude, and it is those things that distinguish or create my experience, my life. There really is nothing else.

I'm trying this out.

I am thinking about what inspires me, really lights me up, and lifts me above *any* circumstances. I'm closing my eyes, letting my mind embrace whatever that might be. Sitting quietly, I let go.

I often look at our employees' lives and the difference our work with Café Gratitude and Sacred Commerce has made in their lives.

I'm opening my eyes now. What was my experience? Was I inspired? Do I feel more buoyant? All I did was shift my thoughts to ones that inspire me. My circumstances haven't changed, yet I shifted my experience of those circumstances in just a few quiet moments of focused thinking. I really feel more inspired. I am seeing how powerful this is.

Now I'm *saying* something out loud, to someone else if possible or to me in the mirror, that acknowledges how amazing I am. I am *saying* it until I feel it, until I can really let this acknowledgment in, deep inside me; I am breathing into it. This is turning out to be more difficult than it sounds.

I practice saying, "I am love, and I am beautiful." I am still working at seeing the beloved in me; it is so much easier for me to see it in others and judge myself.

Now what am I *present* to? What is my experience? Perhaps it is resistance, some internal argument for my smallness. That's okay; it takes practice. I have years of practicing diminishing myself, and if I look, I see my experience of myself is diminished. But when I listen to my affirmations I am able to experience how amazing I truly am. That is how powerful what I am saying to myself and others is.

I can see this is going to take some practice.

I can see myself as the beloved, and the more I practice seeing this the easier it is and the less resistance I have to push through.

Now, I am looking at my *beliefs*. What is a *belief* I have that I have inherited? Perhaps I never consciously chose it; I was just raised with it. I am going to offer an example about relationship, one that I have had for awhile.

In our family once something was broken, or a relationship damaged, it could never be whole again. We could never really get any thing resolved.

How has that *belief* impacted my life? What do I see there? Have I ever questioned my *belief*? What if I could create a new *belief* to replace this old one?

I inherited the belief that a broken relationship was forever damaged, and it had a huge impact on my life, having been sexually abused and divorced before I turned 20. I lived hiding my past, embarrassed and ashamed of who I was. I lied about my past and experienced myself as damaged, inadequate and always trying to compensate for it by proving myself by being a hard worker. Only when I saw that I was passing this crippling and disempowering belief to my children did I awaken and have the courage to fundamentally question it and begin creating something new.

I declare that *beliefs* start out as *thoughts* that I practice for so long they become my *beliefs* – deeply held concepts that, in turn, fuel my other *thoughts*. I do have a choice, however: I can begin practicing a new, empowering *thought*, and if I practice it long enough and deeply enough, it will become a new empowering *belief* of mine.

It took years of practicing that *I am not my personal history*, to start believing that *any thing* can get complete, that Love is the most powerful energy there is! Through Love, I affirm that I am not my history. Rather, I believe that I am who I create myself as now.

What is a new *belief* I would love to believe in?

When I was growing up almost everyone talked somewhat ominously about "when the honeymoon is over," as if those early days of deep love were inexorably destined to end, as if it was unprecedented for two people to sustain the excitement and joy of the relationship called marriage. When Matthew and I were married we created the belief in a "permanent honeymoon" which we practiced thinking, sharing with others and believing as a definite possibility. There is plenty of evidence of relationships changing over time, but what we were committed to keeping alive was the *freshness of discovering one another*, the joy of simply being together. This is the "permanent honeymoon" of kindred spirits and it is our experience. We believe that a *relationship* can be as exciting and as much fun years into it as it was during those early days of falling in love.

Now I am looking at *doing* and asking myself, what is something I do in *relationship* which comes so naturally it seems like it is automatic and is the way I typically participate? Maybe I'm the one who always makes the plans, does most of the driving and usually picks up the tab at the restaurant. Maybe I always take a leadership role at work, or maybe I'm the caretaker, or the passive one. I am selecting something that I struggle with feeling free not to do. I can see that sometimes, although my *actions* may be generous or thoughtful, I feel trapped by them. What if I were absolutely free to do or not to do whatever it might be? Can I see, that once again, the *actions* I take are creating my experience?

I was always the caretaker, tending to the needs of everyone else. It was very difficult for me to do or buy things for myself; I always felt guilty. I had been taught that it is better to give than to receive. I was over 50 before I ever went on a real vacation. I just couldn't spend the money or imagine what I would do. I knew I would feel guilty if I went somewhere without my children and how could I afford to take them? I kept myself busy with work, busy with providing for us. My work defined me, created what I saw as my value. I couldn't imagine spending idle days, doing what? Then Matthew took me to Hawaii, and I found myself swimming in warm sea water and simply relaxing, allowing the Aloha spirit to sink in, for the first time in my adult life. It was wonderful and confronting.

I began to realize that when I let someone else contribute to me, I am actually giving them the gift of giving. Again I had to practice this way of giving so that I could learn that it is valuable to allow others to give just as it is also great to receive. I have received a lot in the past several years, and this has made a huge difference for me. I had to push past guilty thoughts that I was unworthy, undeserving or would be indebted. I have learned to love to give and receive.

Now I am discerning *attitude*. I recall when I was a teenager and my *attitude* was so loud no one could even hear what I was actually trying to say. Perhaps I came home from school one day and my parents just knew I was upset, even though when they asked me how I was, I said, "fine." Maybe my attitude was so loud they chose to just leave me alone for a time, thinking they would check in with me later. *Attitude* can overshadow what I might do, say, or even believe. Its unspoken power is so strong that people don't even have to be near me to detect that something is up. *Attitude* still happens sometimes. I assure my friends and co-workers that I'm fine, when really I'm upset and they know it – they're staying away from me or trying to be especially nice toward me. Sometimes I experience them as trying to make me feel better. We don't have to talk about it; my *attitude* is leaking all over the space.

It can influence everything.

As we are in Oaxaca, Mexico, working on this writing, the world is in the midst of a "financial crisis." Personally, our business has declined for three consecutive months, yet we continue to affirm "*nothing is wrong*." Our bookkeeper e-mailed me this morning, and I could sense his fearful attitude in the e-mail. I wrote back saying, "Consider that we are in the perfect place at the perfect time and are being divinely guided right now." Although we may need to make some changes in our business, I am tuned to trust and faith in knowing that all is well. I can make difficult choices in troubled times and be responsible for my attitude creating an environment of peace and well-being.

I am able to see that it is my thoughts, what I say, the things I do, the beliefs I empower and my attitudes that are creating my experience; it is not my circumstances. I don't have to be a victim of any of these ways of being. I am considering that none are automatic; all are chosen or can be chosen. Certainly I have trained myself to respond to certain situations or events in particular ways, but that's my point. I have trained myself, and I can retrain myself. That's the good news. I am not stuck with anything unless I choose to be.

In *relationship* it is good to consider I never really directly experience another person; I only experience them filtered through my thoughts, speech, beliefs, actions and attitudes, or through my past. Unless I am truly present creating life moment to moment, then my past is my present, and I am often at the effect of it. Everything that a person I am relating to says or does comes through my filter, through the internal "noise" in my head, and is interpreted by me. So the first thing to be responsible for is who *I am being*.

How is *"who am I being?"* impacting what I am hearing and how my friends and loved ones are showing up in my life? I am beginning to see when I take responsibility for my experience I am also more empowered.

Here is something else for me to be responsible for: Am I loving myself? It has been said by many people before me, but it bears repeating, "You can't love anyone else until you love your-self."

This is something I never really understood until I started practicing this view of life. Here is what I see now: if I don't love myself I am simply not present, and love can only be experienced in the present moment.

When I am present I can and do connect with someone else, be in their world and open my world up to them. I am available to give and receive love.

If I were asked, "Where am I not loving myself?" what would I say?

I have come a long way on this one. I can see that it takes daily practice for me to love myself. One area in which I have to consciously shift from judgment to love is in appreciating my aging process – letting go of old ways of comparing myself to others who are usually half my age!

What is that experience like for me? I am seeking to discover: "What is the core feeling I experience when I do not love myself?"

Personally, in that case I feel separate, sad and lonely.

I can see when I am not loving myself I'm stuck in some old story. This signifies that I am either dwelling in the past, with regret and remorse, or fearing the future, living in fear and expectation. I can't *Be Love* for another if I am not here now. In those circumstances, I can't receive love either because love only exists in the present. Therefore, the possibility of love expressing fully between me and anyone else is not available.

How powerful would I "*be*" in *relationship* if I consciously and deliberately chose each and every moment what thoughts I wish to entertain, what I say to myself and others, what actions I might take in any situation, what beliefs I empower, and what overall attitude I might exude in life? I am beginning to see that I would be so powerful that I could create all my relationships as the deep, enriching experiences I am committed to having.

I remember calling out from the bathroom one evening early in our marriage and asking Matthew, "What is something you have never said to me?" thinking he would share some words of love.

He replied, "Well, sometimes I see a hair on your chin and I get hooked by it!" Now that wasn't what I thought I might hear, and although my immediate experience was similar to my breath being taken away, I very quickly felt free. I knew I no longer had to try to pluck my facial hairs in the bathroom mirror when he wasn't looking. Now I am free to pick up the tweezers, walk over to him as he is sitting on our bed and say, "Maybe you can help me pull them out, because I can't always see them anymore."

Practice:
I am practicing what I think, say, believe, do and the attitudes I have.
I am taking on practicing loving myself and others, thinking loving thoughts and saying kind, inspiring things to myself in the mirror. I am also noticing how my beliefs inform my thoughts and words and as a result, I'm choosing only beliefs that inspire me. I am doing everything that supports my being present and maintaining an attitude of gratitude.

When I am upset, it is always because I have replaced reality with illusions I made up. The illusions are upsetting me because I have given them reality, and thus regard reality as an illusion.
—A Course in Miracles

Upsets as My Allies
"What separation thoughts are the source of my upsets?"

Mastery in relationship requires that I understand upsets. For me, the watery world of emotions is a double-edged sword. Often I shape my relationships around the emotions I personally favor: joy, peace, ecstasy and love. I avoid the unpleasant: anger, shame, fear, etc. Consider that emotions are a litmus test for how much *oneness* I am dwelling in, in the moment. If my experience is peaceful, my attention is in the neighborhood of love and trust. This is no big mystery. When my emotional experience is not pleasant, I often place the responsibility outside myself, leaving me a victim of some external circumstance. Upsets are wake-up calls and direction-markers, pointing out where I am being something other then *oneness*.

Upsets are not personal. Freedom lies within. If I can realize that when someone else is upset it's not about their circumstances or the actions of others or myself, I will be well on the way to mastery. If someone in my life is upset, something has activated their wound, their past incompletion, their separation thinking. They are not responding to me. I hold upsets or unwanted emotional experiences like I hold the weather. There is nothing to resist because it is just passing through.

When a child falls and skins her knee I hold that child until the hurt passes. If friends drink themselves into a state of inebriation, I get them to safety, comfort them, and wait out the storm with them. Upsets such as trouble, disquiet and agitation are the weather that is birthed by fragmented thinking. *When I'm upset it's because I've ingested too much separation medicine.* In times like those, all there is to do is have someone hold space for me and wait for the squall to pass. *Being a space-holder for another's upset is terrific training in being present, the best remedy for the patient, and the most loving act in any relationship.*

Upsets, my unwanted emotional experiences, are neither good nor bad; they are atmospheric conditions that are signaling that what I am attending to is something other than love. Upsets are signals telling me where my thinking is off the mark. If used consciously as a tool of awakening, I can celebrate these emotional experiences because they are showing me how the ego is leading me astray. If I'm asleep to the teaching potential of upsets, I can't be grateful for them. The chart that follows is a guide to upsets and what they may indicate about my thinking that maybe hidden from my view. This is not "the truth," but a way of looking at my upsets that may free me to explore my own and support me in holding space for others. These emotional experiences are now my allies, a cause to celebrate. Held this way, they are buoys steering me away from the shackles of my ego. The bigger the upset, the more distorted my thinking, the fouler the weather. I am beginning to see, no matter what, they are only weather.

When I first started doing this work I was completely out of touch with my feelings. I didn't know what I was feeling so I would stop myself many times a day and close my eyes and ask myself, "What am I feeling?" Sometimes my feeling was so foggy to me that the most I could give it was a sound, any sound that came to me. AHHH, OHHH, EEEE, ZAAA. Slowly I began to be able to articulate the feelings. Like a sleuth I began to investigate the upsets and see the fragmented thinking beneath them.

The dark thought, the shame, the malice,
meet them at the door laughing,
and invite them in.
Be grateful for whatever comes,
because each has been sent
as a guide from beyond.
-Rumi, The Guest House

This next section shows examples of *Upsets* and their
corresponding SEPARATION THINKING.

Anger
1. SOMEONE IN MY LIFE HAS VIOLATED ONE OF MY STANDARDS, OR
I HAVE VIOLATED MY OWN STANDARDS.
2. I'M THREATENED. I AM A VICTIM.

Hurt
1. AN EXPECTATION I HAVE HAS NOT BEEN MET.
2. I BELIEVE I'VE LOST SOMETHING.

Disappointment
1. MY INTENTION HAS NOT GONE ACCORDING TO MY PLAN.
2. MY EXPECTATION HAS NOT BEEN FULFILLED. SOMETHING
DIDN'T TURN OUT THE WAY I WANTED IT TO.

Loneliness
1. I CAN'T CONNECT WITH OTHERS OR LIFE. I AM ALL ALONE. NO
ONE KNOWS HOW IT IS FOR ME.

Guilt/Regret
1. I HAVE VIOLATED ONE OF MY OWN HIGHEST STANDARDS.
2. I BELIEVE I AM RESPONSIBLE FOR SOMEONE ELSE.

Fear
1. I AM NOT IN THE PRESENT MOMENT. I AM IN THE FUTURE.
2. I AM EXISTING WITH SOME EXAGGERATED PERCEPTION.
3. I AM AVOIDING AN ISSUE.
4. I AM AVOIDING A COMMUNICATION.
5. I CAN'T HANDLE SOMETHING.

Frustration
1. I'M STOPPED, THWARTED.
2. I DON'T EVER GET A BREAK. IT IS ALWAYS GOING TO BE THIS WAY.

Shame
1. I'M INADEQUATE.
2. I AM BAD, EVIL.

Unworthiness
1. I'M STUPID, LAZY, A PROCRASTINATOR.

Overwhelm
1. THIS IS MORE THAN I CAN DEAL WITH. I CAN'T DO IT.

Grief
1. I AM BEING IMPACTED BY PEOPLE AND EVENTS OUTSIDE MY CONTROL.
2. I HAVE LOST SOMEONE OR SOMETHING IMPORTANT TO ME.

Depression
1. I AM POWERLESS. NOTHING EVER WORKS OUT FOR ME.

Hopelessness
1. WHAT HAS OCCURRED HAS NO VALIDITY, NO MEANING, AND NO LESSON FOR ME.
2. THESE EVENTS ARE AGAINST ME.

Discomfort
1. I AM JUDGING, MEASURING.
2. I AM IN AN UNFAMILIAR PLACE.

Boredom
1. I AM NOT PRESENT. I AM SKIMMING THE SURFACE.

Impatience
1. I AM FEELING NUMB.

*S*pirit is guiding me home with my upsets. I am leaning into them, owning them, being transparent with them, celebrating them, and listening to their message. I don't often look at it this way, but I can hand pick my thoughts; I can practice and create files of love, acceptance, empowerment and peace. The thoughts creating my upsets are a result of my long-standing practice. I can be a victim of my ego's monologue, or I can consciously choose the thoughts I want to entertain. I choose the latter. I am practic- ing it right now. I am closing my eyes, taking a deep breath and repeating aloud, five times, "I am completely fulfilled in this now moment. I am completely fulfilled in this now moment. I am com- pletely fulfilled in this now moment. I am completely fulfilled in this now moment. I am completely fulfilled in this now moment." I'm noticing the shift in my experience, putting my attention on my body and emotions. I'm affirming that it is my thoughts that are the source of my experience. Now I am noticing if I am entertaining any doubting thoughts. Doubt is the mainstay of my ego. Perhaps my ego is already protesting, "This is an affirmation; this is New Age who-ha!" I am noticing that my ego never mocks the power of affirmations when I affirm, "I'm shy, pathetic and unorganized." That's because diminishing affirmations guarantee my ego's survival and my emotional typhoon. Affirmations of wholeness invite my ego to stand down.

I am playing with these possibilities and creating more of my own!

This next section shows examples of
Spirit Qualities/Emotional Experiences and their
corresponding ONENESS THINKING.

Fulfillment

I AM COMPLETELY FULFILLED IN THIS NOW MOMENT.

Peace

I TRUST THAT THE DIVINE ORDER IS DOING ITS PERFECT WORK IN MY LIFE AND EVERYONE'S LIVES.

Joy

I KNOW I AM PERFECT SPIRIT. I KNOW I AM WHOLE AND COMPLETE UNTO MYSELF. I CHOOSE TO BE LOVE AND GIVE, GIVE, GIVE....

Love

I AM ADORING MYSELF. I AM ADORING EVERYONE ELSE. I AM THE ADORING LOVE OF GOD RADIATING FOR MYSELF AND ALL.

Abundance

MY AWARENESS OF THE ALL-PROVIDING NATURE OF SPIRIT IS MY SUPPLY. I AM SPIRIT IN EXPRESSION, AND SPIRIT IS ABUNDANCE. I AM ABUNDANCE.

Gratitude
I AM GRATEFUL FOR WHAT I HAVE. I AM FOCUSED IN THE NOW MOMENT WHERE I HAVE EVERYTHING NOW.

Worthiness
I LOVE AND ADORE MYSELF AS A DIVINE CREATION. I AM WORTHY OF EVERYTHING WONDERFUL.

Terces and I have a paradoxical agreement in our relationship. This is also true among the management at our Café Gratitude restaurants, our family, and close friends. It goes like this.

I am 100% responsible for my emotional experiences, and she is 100% responsible for hers. We are space holders, a safe harbor of acceptance for each to be completely transparent with our upsets and separation thinking. We are always available upon request to apologize to each other if we have left each other in any way diminished and available upon request to acknowledge one another.

At Café Gratitude we encourage employees to bring their upsets to the community for the community to hold. During *the Clearing* (see chapter on clearing) the first question asked is intended to discover the shadow (the distorted thinking) that is the source of the upset or distraction.

In my relationship with Terces, my re-occurring, wounding statement is "I'm not enough," or "I can't do it right." That is what I have practiced, and by this practice I create the upset of shame. Terces' re-occurring, wounding statement is "I'm not heard," or "I don't matter." Her practiced thinking creates the upset of lack of appreciation and frustration. Here is how it looks on the court of our life. We are driving, and Terces looks ahead at the slowing city traffic. Wanting to be helpful she says, "Brake lights," totally neutral. Through my filter of "I'm not enough," I hear, "She thinks I can't drive." If I don't catch myself I might blurt out with attitude, "I actually know how to drive." Now she hears that through her filter of "I don't matter" and she feels frustrated. Now my wound, my distorted thinking, my shame is wrestling with her frustration and her wound. No one is home; no one is present. The key here is to disengage. Usually one of us will recreate (see the chapter on clearing) the other, or one of us will apologize first (see the chapter on apology). I could apologize for indulging in my wound, for activating her wound, for not appreciating her commitment to our safety. She could apologize for speaking in a way that didn't land like an opportunity, for "being right" and finding more evidence for not being heard. It doesn't matter! There is always a reason to apologize! Once we've apologized, we can go to work on cultivating something fresh, creating a new file to *Spiritize* the space. One way we do this is express gratitude to each other for our extraordinary lives.

TREASURE'S STORY

The first year of marriage felt stressful, intense and new. We had all these dreams of a house and children. John had just graduated with his Masters in Business and was intent on helping to build a start-up company. I had recently closed a business into which I had deeply invested my identity. We began to trigger each other's wounds. I behaved in ways I'm not proud of. I screamed and lost control. Then he left me. I went into blaming myself, feeling shame and being devastated. In the clearings at Café Gratitude I was asked questions such as, "how can you take responsibility?", "where can you apologize?", and "who are you making out to be wrong?" I was trained in the practice, the mantra, "I am love, listening to that thought," centering myself in love. But then I started down again – into the shame and inadequacy tunnel.

After being completely out of communication with John, his birthday came along, and I invited him out for tea. He agreed. It was intense to meet up with this man again. Here I had thought I was going to have his children and grow old with him. Instead, we were experiencing our final encounters: negotiating closure, settling money and figuring out how we could share the same friends without running into each other again. My conscious intention for the birthday tea was to Be Love. My internal monologue wanted to make him wrong and judge him for anything he did. I practiced "I am Love, Listening to that thought," and I stayed present. At the tea he asked me, "Why are you here?"

I said, "I want to support you in having an amazing Life!"

"How?" he asked.

"Just by being here with you and celebrating your choices."

This doesn't have a "happy ending" according to ego's grasping and controlling narrative. John and I still don't talk. But I am proud of my ability to be love and to love his choices without resentment, even though they don't include me.

Practice:
"I am love listening to that thought."
I use this mantra to stay centered in love when I perceive
someone is upset with me or critical of me.
Whatever they say, I inwardly say to myself,
"I am love listening to that thought;
I am love listening to that thought."

your fortune is misfortune if it is not Love.
—Silent Lotus

LIFE AS A CLEARING
*"Can I just be here, really listen and
do nothing with it?"*

Clearing is our tool for keeping the past, the wound and the ego from taking control of a relationship. Clearing keeps me present. If I'm not present, I'm in the future (in fear or expectation), or I'm in the past (in guilt, regret and remorse). The Gospel says, "Do not worry about tomorrow, for tomorrow will take care of itself" (Matthew 6:34).

The present is the only place love exists, the only place to give and receive love. I am beginning to see that only the present is real, and it's all I've ever wanted. But my ego sees the present as a threat. It will do anything to keep me out of the present. I notice how much my ego resists meditation or an apology, two other tools I employ to "be" present. Being present is the key to being a *Kindred Spirit*, living in love. It is the key to a workable community. I am realizing that clearing is a practice to keep the space of any relationship open. I see that my clear space calls for vigilance. I am aware that my clear space is always getting filled up with elements of separation; my being present is always being usurped by the past or the future. That's what is so. My toaster makes toast; my ego makes divisions and diversions. And that's okay! My job is to continually clear my space.

CLEARING INSTRUCTIONS:
Preparation. Get myself cleared. This can be done with the first person I clear each day.

First, I "Be with" the person I am clearing. I notice any re-

30.

sistance to looking one another in the eyes. Just "be there;" don't add anything. Take a breath together. That is the Sacred; that is the Love (my word for God) there before me – another human experience. I am being honored and honoring. If I am clearing someone by telephone (yes, it can be done!), I can connect by asking the person if they are ready and committed to being cleared.

I start by asking the person what they are present to. There are many ways I can ask this. At Café Gratitude we choose a different question everyday. The first question deals with the shadow, the wound. This question is designed to distinguish how the habitual mind is creating separation. It begins to cultivate an awareness that one's internal dialogue is just a repetitive mechanism intended to evoke fragmentation.

> **What are you present to?**
>
> **What is in the way of your being here right now?**
>
> **What version of "something's wrong" or "something's missing" are you listening to?**
>
> **What would you love to be forgiven for?**
>
> **What's your biggest disappointment?**
>
> **What's your biggest fear?**
>
> **Who do you gossip about?**
>
> **Where or with whom are you stingy?**
>
> **What are you resisting?**

If the person I am clearing stays conceptual or is talking about something rather then being in their experience, I ask them what that feels like. For example:

Clearer: "What are you present to?"

Being cleared: "I am supposed to go out with my friends tonight, and I don't want to."

Clearer: "What I hear you saying is that you are supposed to go out with your friends tonight, and you don't want to."

Then I ask them: "When your attention is on not wanting to go out with your friends how does that feel or what is that experience like for you?"

Being cleared: "I feel tired and trapped. I don't want to party, and I am afraid they will judge me. And I can see I'm judging my friends."

Clearer: "What I hear you saying is that you feel tired and trapped, you don't want to party, you are afraid of being judged, and you can see you are judging your friends."

Being cleared: "Yes, that's how I feel."

Now the one being cleared is more in their experience. They have moved from their head to their heart.

Listening/Recreation. *I just listen, I don't fix. I recreate what they said verbatim, as in the preceding example. I convey to them that I received their communication. I let them be heard. The fastest way to derail a clearing is to try and "fix" the person being cleared. In the above example, if I had offered advice, such as, "Maybe you could take a nap and join them later," I would have validated the story the person being cleared was inhabiting. I would have moved the attention from their consciousness (something they have control over) to their social circumstances. Such a move would only deepen the illusion that life is about getting the conditions right. Trying to master our circumstances is one cause of scarcity and suffering. Mastering our being is the source of freedom. We do not coach during a clearing.*

Creating something new. This section is an opportunity to shift one's attention to something new. To get present now. To love one's life!

What are you grateful for?

What do you want to be acknowledged for?

What do you love about your life?

What is blessed about your life?

What does your community love about you?

What do you love about your mother?

What moves you?

What inspires you?

If money were no consideration, what would your life be for?

An example:
Clearer: "What do you love about your life?"
Being cleared: "I love that I have the freedom to choose. I love that I am starting to really take care of myself."

This question doesn't necessarily relate to the first one; it isn't a solution or a fix. Sometimes the person being cleared will make a connection. I, however, am not asking the question to better their situation or counteract what they shared previously. I am simply inviting them to shift their awareness.

Acknowledgment. *Next I acknowledge them. I thank them for being there, for their commitment. I let myself be moved. When I am moved they are clear. This is perhaps the most important step.*

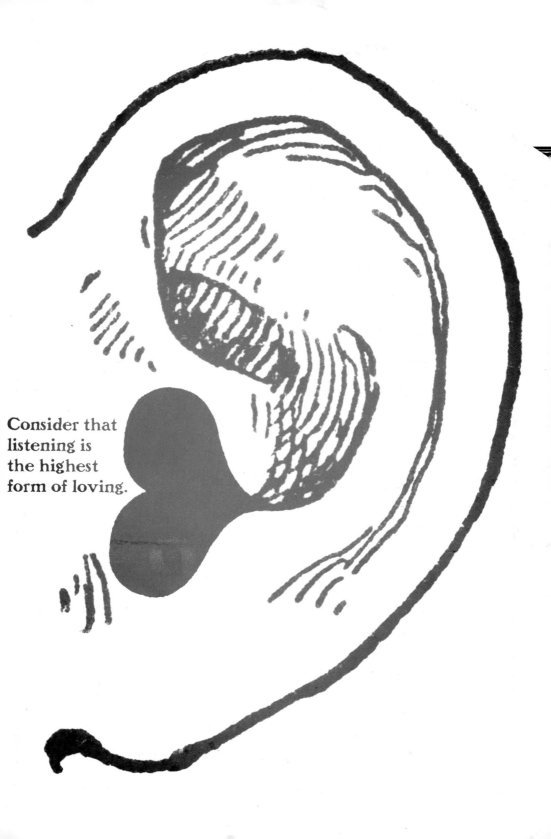

Consider that
listening is
the highest
form of loving.

.ng happens entirely at this point. I am re-
...esn't have to be evidence for acknowledgment.
... is a space that the clearer creates into which the
...red may step. The clearer is invoking a quality of the
...ging it into existence. The clearer's work is to dig deep
ana... moved by the person who is willing to be cleared, thereby dispelling master/servant and higher/lower prejudices and distinctions between clearer and cleared. The clearer is deeply moved by the spiritual being that is having a human experience. Be present to the awareness that they are doing the best they can with the life they have. I acknowledge them. If I am moved by the acknowledgment I can be pretty sure they are clear.

For example:
Clearer: "I would like to acknowledge you. I acknowledge you for being generous, for sharing and giving from your heart. Thank you for being that kind of person. People like you make a difference in the world!"
Being Cleared: I simply let the acknowledgment in.

Clearing is a process that brings me into the present moment and gives me the tools to stay present. If I stay in the present, free of guilt over the past or fear of the future, unconstrained by judgment, what will naturally and automatically arise in my awareness is an experience of Love, Unity, Silence and Peace. These are what I term, *qualities of the Divine*. Clearing is a valuable tool for empowering any relationship or community. It will clear the individual and community distractions that separate it from love. Clearing can be used with great success as a daily practice to realign a community to its mission or restore love to any relationship!

In a "clear" relationship, individuals are not beholden to past mistakes or behaviors. They are complete. Everyone is viewed as a possibility, a consciousness awakening to love.

Awakened relationship is about being responsible for the transformation of one another. Clearing will elicit authentic communication: speaking and listening that will allow a relationship to navigate the upsets and wounds of personalities as opportunities to heal and embrace unconditional love. I often say that *"Listening is the highest form of loving."*

Clearing is a demonstration of this tenet. *Clearing* is the distinct honor of being invited into another's life, having them see that I see how it is for them, and doing nothing with it. When I am in another's world and do nothing with their concern or upset, it disappears. *Clearing* is a sacred ceremony.

Clearing can happen in a group. If I have time I clear one person as an example for everyone to witness. Then people pair up. In the preceding sections we have offered a structure and guidelines. I'm going to use them until I gain a facility for holding space – not fixing, not coaching – just allowing people to see for themselves the source of their distraction. With practice I will be "being a clearing." My inspired life will be sourced from my ability to clear whatever space I inhabit. When I reach the point where I am *"being a clearing,"* every conversation will presence love.

Here is a demonstration of how a clearing could arise naturally during conversation.

Mother/Daughter

Susan: "Hi Mom, how is it going?"

Mother: "Suzy, your father is driving me crazy."

Susan: "What I hear you say is that Dad is driving you crazy."

Mother: "He sits and watches too much television; he's not doing his exercises."

Susan: "He sits and watches too much television; he isn't doing his exercises."

Mother: "The doctor told him he has to walk everyday,

but he doesn't listen to me."

Susan: "You're saying the doctor told him to walk every-day, and he doesn't listen to you."

Mother: "That's right."

Susan: "Mom, when your attention is on Dad not exercis-ing, watching too much television and not listening to you, how does it feel?"

Mother: "I'm frightened of becoming a widow, of being left alone, and I feel as though your father doesn't care about me or about living."

Susan: "What I hear you saying is that you are frightened of becoming a widow, of being left alone, and that you feel as though Dad doesn't care about you or about living."

Mother: "Yes, that's how I feel."

Susan: "Mom, can I ask you another question?"

Mother: "Sure."

Susan: "What would you like to be acknowledged for?"

Mother: "Honey, I don't need to be acknowledged."

Susan: "Really, Mom. I could acknowledge you for many things, but what would you love to be acknowledged for?"

Mother: "For always seeing the glass as half full instead of half empty."

Susan: "Mom, I want to completely acknowledge you and celebrate you for always seeing the best in life and the best in others. For always seeing the glass half full instead of half empty. You passed your optimism on to me, and I thank you. "Mom, how do you feel now?"

Mother: "I love you honey."

Friend/Upset Friend

Joe: "Hey, how's it going?"

Josh: "I've got a bone to pick with you."

Joe: "You've got a bone to pick with me? What's up?"

Josh: "Where the heck have you been? When you relocated, you moved in and slept on my couch for weeks. I loaned you money and then you just disappeared."

Joe: "I'm hearing you say that I disappeared after moving in, sleeping on your couch for weeks and taking money you loaned me."

Josh: "Yeah."

Joe: "So Josh, when you're thinking about me living with you, taking the money you loaned me and not coming around, how does that feel?"

Josh: "I feel abandoned and conned. I'm distrustful and angry."

Joe: "What I hear you saying is that you feel abandoned, conned, distrustful and angry. Anything else?"

Josh: "Nope, that's it."

Joe: "Josh, I want to apologize for leaving you with the experience of being conned or in away diminished. I understand that I left you with that. I have been so in my head about not finding a job; I've felt so ashamed about not being able to pay you back. I've been afraid of your reaction. I've been avoiding you and I apologize. Please accept my apology. Do you have any requests of me?"

Josh: "Apology accepted. My request is that you make a commitment to repaying me, even if it's only five dollars a week. And let's hang out some."

Joe: "Thank you Josh, I accept your request. It's really good to see you."

Josh: "I can see now that part of my anger and distrust was due to me thinking that I'd made a new friend and then lost him."

Joe: "I felt like that too. I thought I'd blown our friendship. Thanks for understanding."

Practice:
*I am choosing a clearing partner and we are practicing clearing
every day together.*

If the beloved is everywhere, the lover is a veil, but when living itself becomes a friend, lovers disappear.

—Rumi

FALLING IN LOVE WITH MYSELF
"What would I have to give up to fall head over heels in love with myself?"

I am considering that I am my own worst enemy, that my judgment of myself is the biggest obstacle in my relationships. The word sin is derived from a Greek archery term, meaning "to miss the mark." Divine Love is the bull's eye and anything else – anything that distracts me from that mark, is a sin. When I criticize myself, I am in a sense sinning. I am missing the mark. Self-criticism signifies that I am following false gods, something other than Christ consciousness, something other than unconditional love. As Mother Theresa said, "Even God cannot fill what is already full." If I don't love myself then I've created myself as deficient, in which case I can't be love or radiate love. Instead, love becomes something I'm out to "get." Then I project this deficiency on to my partners and my community, and they fall short. I can't even receive love from another unless I am being love. Here's an example:

Terces and I are in Oaxaca writing this book. Earlier today we were in a beautiful local market full of food and flowers and culture. Terces was being effusively in love with Mexico and with me and talking to every mamacita and showing me every little nuance of this splendid country. I found her enthusiasm annoying. She was clearly being love but I was dominated by fear of a financial situation back in the USA. I couldn't be present to her love because I was worshiping **F.E.A.R.** (**F**alse **E**vidence **A**ppearing **R**eal, also known as **F**orgetting **E**verything is **A**ll **R**ight). Love is not there!

If love is a presence and a consciousness that I can invoke

through my thoughts, speech, beliefs, actions and attitudes, then there is no absence of love. The lack is in my attention, the only thing I have any control of. To invoke love's presence, to be the source of my own love experience, is a key to successful relationship. The basis for that is my gratitude for my life. I am starting by practicing loving myself.

Practices for Loving Myself

1. I will do things for myself I wouldn't normally do, like getting a massage once a week, taking belly dancing classes or anything that I have wanted to do for myself that I know is good for me but that shyness or feelings of inadequacy have kept me from doing.

2. I will dare to make requests of others that are a stretch for me. This is an exercise in my worthiness. I remember that "no" doesn't mean anything, so I collect "no's" as an exercise in my worthiness. I make requests such as, "Will someone be my clearing partner?", "Will you go out on a date with me?", "May I have a raise in my pay?", and "Will you take me with you on that cruise you're going on?"

3. I will ask people to acknowledging me. "I'd like to be acknowledged for......."

4. I will adore the person I see in the mirror. I will hug myself, kiss myself and say out loud (for example), "I am a Divine masterpiece. I love and admire myself. I am Spirit revering itself!"

5. I will have the "hard" conversations with other people that I am avoiding as an exercise in being heard and worthy.

6. I will create dates with myself, light candles, take time out for an especially soothing bath, meditate in a sacred space; give myself quality time.

7. I will get cleared everyday.

And now here is my secret, a very simple secret; it is only with the heart that one can see rightly, what is essential is invisible to the eye.
—Antoine de Saint-Exupery

DISCOVERING EACH OTHER
Who am I creating you as?

I remember when I first began to truly explore the idea that a person wasn't any way in particular, but that, in actuality, how they were showing up in my life was based on how I was creating them. I began to notice how my opinions and judgments of others were creating my experience. Once I saw that, I felt liberated. That's when I knew I didn't have to be stuck with any experience of another person, because I was free to to develop my ability to see the best in everyone, to create them as an expression of love. Wow, that was exciting! It turned out to be challenging, as well.

I started with my mother. Certainly I had told myself she was a certain way. I noticed that I took her phone calls and telephoned her in return more out of obligation and a sense of duty, than of joy. Sure, I loved her, but I didn't always want to talk with her. Looking at what I was creating, I saw that the reason I didn't always look forward to speaking with her was because of my own sense of inadequacy, the experience of not being enough for her. This was coming through my filter – that she thought I should be doing more for her or being better toward her in whatever area of life I was currently sharing with her. I also saw that I didn't really listen to my mom. In the role I assigned her, "she said the same thing over and over again" and was "in her own world" and not related to mine.

After seeing this, I became courageous and shared with her what my experience of her was. I apologized for how I had been creating her.

Her reply was so very generous. She told me, "I always think you are doing too much, and that you work too hard. I wish you would take better care of yourself. I miss you. I would love to see you more, but you're so busy. I don't know how you do all you do."

Suddenly, I experienced my mother in a different way. I felt connected to her, proud of her, grateful for her being in my life. What had changed? I connected and shared myself with her. From then onward I started listening to my mom, and the more I truly listened the more I discovered what an amazing woman she was. Matthew and I cared for her in her last years. I discovered more about who she was in those years than all the previous years when I thought I knew who she was. Looking through the eyes of love I see love. Now as the years go by since her death, I see so much of what she taught me coming out in my own actions. I have such a deep appreciation for her talents, her skills, her efforts and her expressions of love and caring.

Early in our relationship, I was visiting my son's house and I noticed my childhood Bible. I took it and flipped through familiar pages. I came to the few pictures at the back that I had spent hours looking at as a child, and instantly I had a deep awareness that I loved Matthew the way I love Jesus. Tears ran down my cheeks. I was experiencing the same unconditional love for them both. I have cultivated that awareness and kept it blooming in our relationship. I even acknowledged my awareness in my wedding vows. Of course, not everyone experiences Matthew the way I do. It isn't necessarily true that he is any particular way, but for me he shows up as a powerfully committed man, who loves unconditionally, whom I love unconditionally, like I love Jesus. One love.

I am considering that I learn about others first, from what is shared about their lives, about who they say they are. Next, what is being said goes through my filter, my thoughts and experiences of them. I can see that once I get to know you through my filter it would be difficult for me to experience you any other way. In fact, I'll keep putting you in the same old box and relating to you like you are a certain way, even setting you up to continue to show up exactly as I already know you to be.

There isn't anything "wrong" with that model of relationship; it's just that it's inhibiting.

Now I am telling myself to be "realistic;" everyone in my life isn't great. It would be completely inauthentic for me to think that they all are just terrific. So I'm looking at that. Have I ever met someone and fallen in love? I remember those first few days, weeks or months, when everything they said or did was amazing. Was my experience of them authentic? Yes? Okay, let's fast-forward six months, perhaps a year and, *voila*! I can hardly stand them any longer. In fact, I avoid going to places that I know they frequent, just in case I might run into them there. Is that authentic? I am beginning to consider that it is all made up! My experience of them is my interpretation.

Here's the big question: if I'm making it all up anyway, why not make up things about myself and other people that empowers us?

Here's what I choose to make up: the only authentic *expression* of anyone is unconditional love. Everything else is just my resistance to *being* love, and that's what I can see is not authentic.

What if I really could *discover* someone else each and every day? What if I could hold a space open for them to show up in and use my gift of acknowledgment to call them into being, to bring forth the qualities that we all aspire to? How wonderful would that be?

Practice:
I am practicing creating everyone in my life as great, seeing them all as love (consciousness awakening). I am practicing saying to myself as I walk through life, "I am in love with you, and we are in love together."

What I love about me is you.
—Mark Edwards

The Gift of Acknowledgment
What divine quality am I calling forth?

"Acknowledgment," as I think most of us know it, is crediting someone for something they have done. Although that is great, it is not what I am talking about here.

When we were working with the Priests in Mexico, training them in clearing, one of the Fathers said, "If Jesus came back today, he would say, "Blessed are those who affirm."

This is what I am referring to as *acknowledgment*: the affirmation in another person of a quality of the Divine, the invocation of their greatness. Imagine if I looked at anyone, everyone and what I saw was the *blessed* in them? Guess what? It's there! I even have plenty of evidence for this. Look at my life: I see that when someone relates to me like I am magnificent, I step up to that. I become more magnificent. In fact, I struggle to act in magnificent ways and not give into something less than that. Just like if, on the other hand, someone treats me like I can't be trusted, I step down to that, and pretty soon I will act in ways that are deceitful. *Kindred Spirit* pertains to developing my ability to see love expressing in and as everyone; to summon it, acknowledge it and then hold space for it while love shows up. Consider if I could master this, I would be living in the presence of the Divine all the time.

I can take on acknowledging people anytime, anywhere. This is not an evidence-based act; it is an act of faith. "For we walk by faith, not by sight" (II Corinthians 5:7). When I have faith, and I believe, then I see. So I start by believing in the love of everyone, and I start seeing it.

I can acknowledge a person for any quality or way of being; therefore I choose those qualities that inspire me. This is essential to transforming my relationships. I begin to transform how I see them, and I begin to be responsible for who I am creating them to be.

I can not only start acknowledging everyone, I can also practice requesting to be acknowledged, which is just as miraculous. Imagine the freedom to say to a loved one, boss, or friend, "I would love for you to acknowledge me for being committed (or any divine quality or virtue)," and then really let in the acknowledgment I receive. Keeping the acknowledgment in the form of *being* is important, otherwise I quickly slip back into our evidence-based, doing existence.

When Matthew and I were last in Mexico, our workshop was attended by researchers from Mexico's Department of Agriculture. It was quite a challenge for some of them. First of all, their work and training were all evidence-based, and they felt like the only place a faith-based approach that was appropriate was in church. They could only imagine acknowledging for a job well done. So we gave them the homework of acknowledging their wives and children as part of the practice. They ran into resistance and skepticism from their families, along lines of "you don't need to acknowledge me," or "what do you want?," and "what have you been drinking?" It was so foreign for their loved ones to be acknowledged, let alone for them to request acknowledgment. Suspicion and mistrust arose to be healed, not only culturally, but from years of acknowledgment being absent. It was several days into the workshop before they were finally able to experience the value of being acknowledged themselves, which led to them seeing the value of practicing it in other areas of their lives.

It is sad really that I have drifted so far from seeing and calling forth the greatness in others, I am encouraged to take on this practice of becoming an expert at acknowledging everyone, for no reason. It will transform my life and community.

What if seeing the Divine in everyone is my highest expression?

Practice:
With a partner I practice acknowledging them and use active listening as I am being acknowledged.
This isn't looking for something to acknowledge.
It isn't the truth; there isn't proof. I don't go to the past; I invent them anew, create from nothing, and then they step into it. I am creating a world in my speaking, and they rise up to that.
Now we trade places.
Now I go back and ask my partner what they would like to be acknowledged for. I take on practicing active listening and then acknowledge them for what they shared! We trade places again.
What is my experience?
Where do I get stopped in acknowledging?

47.

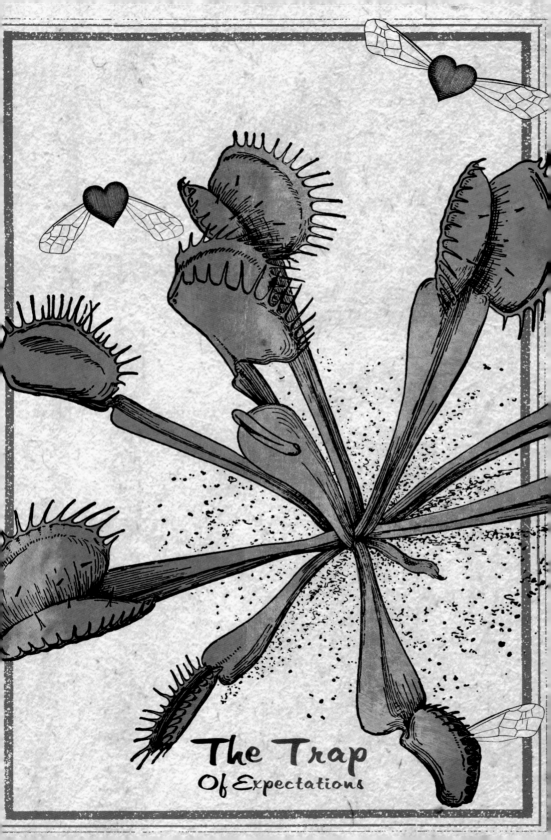

The Trap
Of Expectations

Expectations suck the joy out of life.
—Sri Sri Ravi Shankar

THE TRAP OF EXPECTATIONS
Am I a request for love or expressing love?

Nothing I know of diminishes my experience as much as expectation. I simply set myself and others up to fail when I hold or place expectations on them or on life itself. When I'm living in expectation, I'm not present either, since expectations always live in the future, in what hasn't happened yet. Even if life responds by fulfilling my expectations, all I have is the simplest of satisfactions because underneath most expectations lurks some version of the hungry ghost. When my attention is wanting, I get more wanting, and I keep having more expectations. When someone does what I expected, then I expect it again in the future. When the day comes that my expectations are not fulfilled, then I am upset.

I'm looking to see if my expectations are actually requests that I have not powerfully made, some hopeful future not powerfully caused or intended. I am afraid to ask for what I desire, so I silently expect it, hoping it will happen. When my expectation is fulfilled, I am happy. When it isn't, I am upset. Neither experience is powerful, for I am teaching myself that happiness and satisfaction lies "out there," in the results or circumstances of life.

Real power is found by realizing that whatever experience I am having I am the one creating it. My disappointment in an unfulfilled expectation is not coming from "out there" somewhere; neither does it rest with someone else who "failed me." Rather it is mine; I am the one creating it. In having expectations there is no room for the miraculous or the extraordinary to show up, only for my expectation to be fulfilled or not.

I used to hope that Matthew would write me love letters. I would look forward to my birthday or Christmas in the expectation of some sweet words on a piece of paper. But the letters didn't show up. As a result, I would experience some sadness and disappointment. After one such experience I said to him, "I would love for you to write me love letters."

He replied, "Is that a request?"

I said, "Yes." Occasionally he sends me an email, or leaves a note, and when I made my request repeatedly as my birthday approached this year, he wrote me a card. I no longer experience sadness. I can make the request, sometimes more than once, and he will write me. Or I simply let go of my expectation and be present to all the wonderful ways he does indeed express his love for me that often exceed any expectation I might have had.

Practice:
What is an expectation I have that I could turn into a powerful request?
Now, I will make that request.

Your task is not to seek for love, but merely to seek and find all the barriers within yourself that you have built against it.
—Rumi

MAKING POWERFUL REQUESTS
What do you need to hear from me to restore love to our relationship?

In our Café Gratitude restaurants we found ourselves making our servers and managers wrong for coffee drinks that were delivered to a table without a spoon. We made the request that they get that aspect of table service into the training. Even so, sometimes we still notice that coffee will go out without spoons and we speak up, point it out, and make another request that we get that into the training.

I can make a powerful request and then notice that I've set myself up for a new expectation. Conversations go out of existence; they can fade from memory. They are not tangible. I don't tell someone I love them only once and then never say it again. In the same sense, I often need to repeat my requests over and over again.

Requests are actually opportunities to empower others, to let someone know what I want or need, to support them in doing a great job or fulfilling their desire to excel or please.

Often times the reason I don't make requests is that I don't want to experience "rejection" by hearing "no" for an answer. I am considering that if I never make the request I live in some level of fear, afraid of the "no." I am remembering, however, that "no" doesn't mean anything; it isn't personal. *No only means, not now!* It doesn't signify all the other disheartening baggage that I add to

51.

it, such as, "you don't love me; you reject me; I'm not important; my ideas aren't good; what I think isn't important." I am the one adding all the extra meaning and upsetting myself in the process. I am seeing that "no" simply means "no" – nothing else.

Here's something miraculous. I say if I become a master at hearing "no" and not adding any meaning to it, I will be one of the most powerful people on the planet! Getting a "no" directs me, guides my progress, and sends me in other directions seeking a "yes" or altering my request.

Practice:
I am making a powerful request of someone in my life that is difficult for me. My request is stretching me outside of my comfort zone.
I am practicing that "no" doesn't mean anything except "no."
I am seeing how many no's I can get on a daily basis.
I am making lots of requests.

What could there be to fear in a world that I have forgiven and that has forgiven me?
—A Course In Miracles

LETTING GO OF BEING RIGHT. A COMMITMENT TO KINDNESS

"With whom in my life am I more committed to being right then being kind?"

Being right and being love can't occupy the same space. I am considering that my insistence on being right is an addiction, and like any addiction, being right creates an alternative reality, an alternative to love. Wars are fought, families are destroyed, opportunities are squandered, friends are abandoned – all in the name of being right. Being right is a mainstay of the ego's machinery. The Dalai Lama, whose religion is kindness, has lots of evidence for being right about the Chinese atrocities, but he doesn't fall for the ego's trickery. Being right and enlightenment are incompatible. His commitments are not distracted by the intoxication of righteousness. In "being right" I trade Divine Love for self-righteousness. Being right only creates positions. Someone's on the attack, and someone's defending and justifying. When a relationship is caught in the *bardo* of attack-and-defend, the only way out is for either party to surrender, to relinquish their position, to be more invested in workability then divisiveness.

I am getting present to the impact that insisting on being right has had on my life. Until I see where being right has killed off relationships, I might not be motivated to surrender my position. Being right is against the flow of the entire universe. It is an exhausting drain upon my aliveness and a detriment to my health. "Being right" guarantees that I will continue to live in my head, as

I continually justify my position, at the exclusion of my heart. Why does so much healing work (the surrendering of positions) happen among people who are sick and dying? The arrogance of the ego's reign is often overcome when we're facing the end of life. But why wait? As Rumi observed, "You set out to find God, but then you keep stopping for long periods at mean-spirited road houses."

Practice:

With whom in my life is love not as present as it once was? What am I being right about? What is the cost of that position on me, my family, and my community? Does my position forward love and oneness or multiply the illusion of separation? Is my position worth the absence of love?

I am remembering I don't give up being right for someone else (and it very well might inspire them if I did). I am liberating myself from my ego's enslavement and returning my conscious-ness to love. Consider that forgiveness means to give as before. I understand that we all are caught in physicality; we all have made fear, death, loneliness and abandonment real. Through the eyes of forgiveness I see all "sins" (actions that miss the mark of love) as equal. I see the ego as an overwhelming illusion and understand how all of us get led astray. Ultimately I forgive myself and others for entertaining anything other then love.

CHANDRA'S STORY

A much loved Café Gratitude employee and long-standing friend of mine had a boyfriend with whom she broke up. Unknown to her, her manager at Café Gratitude started going out with her former boyfriend. On discovering this, the employee reacted to this perceived outrage with such turmoil and fury that she was fired from her position, the police were summoned, and she was banned from our café. Our human resource consultant strongly advised me to leave this alone and not to attempt to resolve it. Our job, the consultant advised, was to keep our manager safe. Yet, I just couldn't see how this laissez-faire approach was serving the whole. I was committed to getting this situation complete and restoring love. I leaned into the discomfort, held space for everyone to have their experience, and patiently waited for our two beloveds to be ready to meet. A meeting was finally held; both our current employee and our former employee took the opportunity to inhabit each other's world. As a result, they were both able to take responsibility and apologize. They asked each other, "What do you need to hear me say to restore love to this relationship?" And love was restored.

Practice:
I am taking on leaning into the discomfort.
I am holding space for everyone to have their experience.

I can escape from this by giving up attack thoughts.
—A Course In Miracles

IF I WANT COMFORT I'LL GET A DOG
"Why am I in relationship?"

My predominate context for having a relationship is and has been security, comfort, validation and camaraderie. I look for someone to remedy my sense of aloneness, inadequacy and scarcity. I fall in love with my new partner, new friend, new boss. I create that I am secure or loved and project that love and perfection outward; I see through the eyes of love. Everything about them is perfect; life even looks perfect through the glasses worn during this fantasy stage. It is completely made up, invented. Not right, not wrong, just created. As time passes my ego's judgment begins to supersede my conscious generation of love and my new relationship loses its luster. Now I know how they are: perhaps they're annoying or I can only stand them in small doses. My ego's ugliness is projected outward and I either break up with them or we tolerate each other based on co-dependency. Again, I made all that up; I created it. Both are valid views of that person. One invokes joy, excitement and love; the other boredom, indifference, disappointment, and sometimes even rage. And so the cycle goes on and on. I keep looking for "the one."

What if the one I am looking for is really the One, the one consciousness expressing as many? What if love is a presence – a state of mind? What if *relationship* is about awakening to this realization? What if life is an inside job, and what I am hoping that a relationship can fulfill can only be attained in my awareness? What if my relationships fail because I place expectations on my partners they cannot fulfill? I consider that the universe (the one song) would be doing me a huge disservice if it had me find fulfillment

If You Want

COMFORT

Get A Dog.

anywhere other then in the abode of my heart. My human thirst is never quenched in the outer. As a *Kindred Spirit* I understand that I am the writer, director and star of my movie. I am making it all up, and I am willing to use relationship as a means to discover how my screenplay is prohibitive to my expression of unconditional love.

"Are we using this relationship to awaken together?" Imagine if this was my standard question on a first date, a job interview, a tenant/landlord inquiry, the prelude to the blessing at my family's Thanksgiving dinner. My ego finds this threatening.

Transparency is an endangerment to my machinery, the ego-mechanism that is sure that if you really knew who I am you would flee. Being a *Kindred Spirit* requires that I tolerate the discomfort of self-disclosure and *be acceptance* for however the shadow expresses in myself and others. Wherever I am defending a secret, love cannot penetrate. That's why, when I reflect on the stereotype we have of relationships in our society, I remind myself, "If I want comfort I should get a dog."

This is not a "cozy" path! There is no vitality in the "comfort zone"; *safe is a sedative*. I'd rather lean into the discomfort. In this book I am being trained to generate my own love experience, to say the hard things, to create an environment for being transparent, to speak in a way that lands in another's world like an opportunity.

Our son Ryland is always calling me out to be my highest self. If I am being funny, soliciting admiration, at the expense of others he will say, "So Dad, are you being love or asking for love?" He is my Kindred Spirit; the context of our relationship is that he is my Zen master, there to remind me that I am whole and complete and that my "need" for validation doesn't reach my majesty.

Practice:

I am creating conscious contexts for three important relationships in my life. I am going to share them with those people and ask them if they agree to play that game.
If not we will create a context together.

Examples:

1. Our relationship is a safe space to say anything and hear anything without judgment.

2. I'll see the Christ presence in you and you'll see the Christ presence in me.

3. Let us each be the other's hero.

4. We are love courageously expressed in the World.

5. We won't let each other diminish ourselves.

6. I'll make sure your life is great; you make sure my life is great.

If we really want to love
we must learn to forgive.
—Mother Teresa

APOLOGY AND GETTING COMPLETE
What if no aspect of my past was holding me back?

Living in regret keeps me from being present as regret always lives in the past, and I remember love can only be given and received in the present. Apology is an opportunity to end any regret. To stop blaming myself or someone else for any experience I may be having, apology is the way. In every situation I can take 100% of the responsibility and apologize for any break in love. It isn't necessarily true that I am 100% responsible, but it is a powerful place for me to stand. Any other place has me be a victim, or otherwise incomplete. My apology isn't always a request for forgiveness, but it may be. It isn't even necessary for me to be forgiven; an apology can be complete within itself.

Last year I had the realization that the father of two of my children, and the grandfather of my three granddaughters, was very likely still blaming himself for our divorce. I thought about what his life must have been like 32 years ago, having just returned from the Viet Nam war, dealing with drug addiction and struggling to create a life with me in Pennsylvania on a farm. I, too, had been lost – in abuse and addiction – and last year it dawned on me that I had never really apologized to him for my part in our struggles. I had never said to him, "I don't blame you."

So I phoned him and I told him, "I don't blame you," and he began to weep and I could sense the wave of relief that swept over him. He in turn apologized for the way he had treated me. He had not known how to be any other way. He shared that since last I spoke with him he had gone to prison on a domestic violence rce. I thoug...

diction and then strugg... never really apo...

...I realized I had never really apo...

...him just that and he started crying, I could...

...how to be any other way. He shared...

...t know how to be any other way. He also said tha...

...help him deal ... his anger. He said that he was cele...

...any requests of ... Matthew, my...

...seen ... children...

birthday p... said it was the...

te his birthday...

a very healing experien...

lationship for me...

GETTING COMPLETE

...is a declara... else should be...

charge and that now he was attending in a course in anger management. He also said that the Veterans Administration was finally helping him after all these years. I asked if he had any requests of me. He said that he was celebrating his 60th birthday this year and that he would love it if the kids and I would attend his party. I said we would. Matthew and I, and three of our children, two of their spouses and all three grandbabies traveled to celebrate his birthday. He had only seen his children a few times in their lives and had never seen his grandchildren. It was a wonderful, fabulous trip and a healing experience. He informed us that it was the best birthday present he ever could have hoped for. Now there is nothing incomplete in my relationship with him, and all this due to the power of apology!

Being complete is a declaration. It is something I declare and there need not be any evidence for it. I simply stop creating the attitude that "something is missing," that something else should be present. I say what I have to say, request what I want, apologize, forgive or take whatever action completes the situation for me, regardless of how it is received or reciprocated. Then I declare it whole and complete.

CORIE'S STORY

My dad and mom got a divorce when I was around 9 or 10 years old. I don't actually remember my dad being around much from around age 5. For years after he left, I could not understand why it was so difficult for him to call or to write me a letter or to remember my birthday. These things I decided a parent should automatically do. I was angry with him for 25 years. I became completely resolved to erase him from my life, just as I felt he had done to me. I became aware that this resolution was not workable, however, in that feelings of anger, longing and sadness kept arising in me, repeatedly. What I saw was that my anger was my protection against being vulnerable and being hurt again. I wanted my dad to love me, but I didn't want to lean into the discomfort and risk what I perceived to be the awkwardness involved in reconnecting with him. Eventually I chose different thoughts, and I picked up the phone one day and spoke with him. I apologized to my dad for the years of anger and resentment that I had held towards him and that I had obstructed the potential for us to have a relationship. I could hear him crying on the other end of the line...this big, hard-working, rugged man was on the phone with me weeping at the words that I was offering to him. I realized at that moment what I had stolen from him. I also became aware of the power of apology and taking responsibility for my own behavior.

What our relationship looks like now isn't actually that drastically different; however, the mutual sensitivity and feeling of the relationship is very much improved! We talk almost every other week, which is something that has never happened. The biggest shift for me is that although he still does not call me consistently, although he still hasn't written a letter, I am sitting in my seat completely aware that he loves me and cherishes me, and I no longer make the silent phone or empty mailbox signify rejection or some other old story. The gift that he and I gained from *apology* is a gigantic clear space of love and affection.

Practice:

I am apologizing all the time. I take responsibility for what I say and how it lands in another's world. If there is static or an unclear space in any of my relationships I am looking at how I am responsible and what I can apologize for. This is not the truth but the only place I can stand in power. I often ask, "What do you need to hear to restore love to this relationship?"

Giving
Living
Loving
100%
with NO
expectation

In real love you want the other person's good.
In romantic love you want the other person.
—Margaret Anderson

FREEDOM OF NON ATTACHMENT-GIVING, LIVING AND LOVING 100% WITH NO EXPECTATION
What would love do now?

What is it really like to love someone and at the same time not be attached to them? Is it even possible? It appears to be an insurmountable paradox. Loving someone seems to imply that I have picked them; I would also be invested in the fact that they have chosen me. How do I stay unattached in a situation as intimate and passionate as that?

It's difficult to see what is possible in relationship when I keep looking at it from my same old viewpoint. I could say, "Of course I'm attached! This is the person I love! I don't want anything to happen to our relationship that would alter it or cause me to forfeit it."

Let's step back a bit and see if I can look at this from another perspective. Can I see that of course I want my relationship to change, grow, deepen and mature? Of course I want to continue to discover even more magnificence in my partner! I have chosen a new, sun-ripened thought: if I'm attached to the relationship, I'm stifling it. It's a bit like hoarding money, which cuts off my flow of abundance. A healthy relationship is an organic process that is constantly changing. In fact, I'm the one who is changing it; I'm the one who continues to strengthen my ability to create it as even more amazing. I'm the one who manages to keep my attention on all that is wonderful about it, all that is healing, fulfilling and transformative, all that weaves the beautiful tapestry that constitutes the blossoming and awakening of each person in the relationship. Otherwise, I'm in some way attempting to control the relationship. One day such a controlling practice will end up being unfulfilling, and we will become numb to one another. I am seeing that I want someone cheering me on; and I in turn want to champion my partner.

I want what Matthew wants, and he wants what I want. Early in our relationship, I said to Matthew, who is always noticing beautiful women, "There are plenty of amazing women you could be with, but you would be crazy to be with anyone else, I'm your girl!" He has shared with me that just allowing him to have his vision of other women, to not be threatened because he enjoys noticing feminine beauty, to be that certain and confident of my love for him, has set him free, allowed him to be himself and be *present* to our love. It has set me free because I know I am the woman he continually chooses to share his life with.

If I am attached to what my relationship looks like I am cutting off the creation of it, the chaotic moments of death and birth. I will start protecting and defending my relationship rather than breathing into the expansion of love.

Cary's Story

A friend of mine tells me that beginners luck is really as simple as not knowing what to be afraid of. When it came to my first romantic relationship of my adult life I was truly lucky. Not only had I found an amazing romantic partner, but also a woman who would end up teaching me some of the most valuable lessons of my life.

I met Megan on my first day of work at Café Gratitude. It was also her first day, and she offered to let me copy her "notes" that she was taking while training. The fact that she was taking notes on a little piece of paper made me laugh and adore her all at once. She was beautiful, confident and also regrettably funnier than me. Megan and I quickly became best friends and then started dating. We worked together and lived together, sharing most of the day in each other's presence. We were partners in crime and love mischief.

I learned a lot in my relationship with Megan, such as how to accept upsets and truly communicate in a way that helped us both see what was at the heart of any disagreement. Before my relationship with Megan I had avoided upsets, but now I was seeing them as an opportunity to grow.

After four years of dating Megan I began to get frightened. I was 24 years old at the time and I was starting to create my relationship as a trap. I felt like I had found my perfect partner too early and that it was limiting me from exploring the rest of the world and other relationships freely. It was a shameful experience for me, and I was scared to communicate it to anyone. This put a strain on the undercurrent of our relationship. I didn't know what to do. I yearned for a way to make everything work and be comfortable.

During this time Megan began spending time with one of our mutual friends. Her relationship with this man eventually turned romantic. Megan admitted to me what was happening, and of course I was crushed. I felt betrayed. I trusted her, and I had trusted the friend with whom she had become intimate. I had felt proud of myself for trusting them, and when I was informed that this trust had been taken advantage of, it hurt more than I could imagine. Megan and I broke up, and I went through days of difficult thoughts and anger. Megan was continuing to live and work with me. She was still employed as my parents' personal assistant. Being around all of this was overwhelming.

Noticing what my head was doing, and what my heart was feeling, I came to a realization that changed my life forever. I loved Megan. I still love Megan. Since that's the case, do I want her to experience any day on this planet not feeling like she is loved and cared for? Certainly not. What is obstructing my ability to forgive her? If I really searched, the only thoughts I could come up with

were: "She deserves to suffer! It's her fault! Forgiving her is letting her off easy!"

All of these thoughts drifted through me, but I was clear I was not committed to them. I could choose to indulge in them and feel very justified, or I could choose something more empowering for Megan and myself.

I knew that my forgiveness of Megan was inevitable. I didn't see any benefit for her or for me to delay it. I met with her, and I forgave her and let her know that I loved her. Although we were no longer going to be together romantically, I wanted her to be in my life. After feeling surprisingly clear about this choice, I got hit with another surprise. Soon after I forgave Megan, I became overwhelmingly inspired. I became conscious that I was a 24-year-old male, and I was not a jerk! What a relief! I had experienced my first heartbreak, and I had transformed it into an opportunity. I had been able to take what appeared to be a heart-breaking mess and through forgiveness transform it into a feeling that empowered and inspired me. In retrospect, my choice to forgive Megan was selfish. I wanted to feel good again. I knew I would not feel complete with our relationship if I was carrying around resentment for her.

While I was on my forgiveness high, I decided to keep it going and forgive my friend who Megan had cheated on me with. My forgiveness of him did not come as easy as my forgiveness with Megan, and took more time before I was comfortable with it. I couldn't help but see all of these conversations as a huge training opportunity for me. I had always been told by my mother that we can create the reality that we live in – that we can choose our experience. I believed her conceptually, but this was the first time I had experienced it. I began to feel unstoppable. I was young, and I had so much to look forward to: Arguments with future lovers, crying, disappointment, debt, divorce, more crying.

The next few weeks that passed were some of the most inspiring days of my life. I felt mature and powerful. I stopped being so afraid of what loss the future might bring, and I knew that there was nothing for me to fear. I now felt better prepared to meet my life's future challenges and transform into something that serves me. With this out of the way, I was more present in my life. Megan is still in my life today as one of my most dear friends. I love her unconditionally and call on her for support when I get stuck. I feel lucky to call her my first love.

If I am attached I start to think that love is out there, in that body, with that person. What I am saying is love is a presence, and I can presence it anywhere, anytime, with anyone.

I notice it in my life when Matthew and I have something planned, some time together. I start to imagine how it will be; looking forward to some experience, I start to script and anticipate it in my mind. Then I overhear Matthew invite someone else to come along, maybe even a few people. I notice my heart starts to close. I give myself the experience of disappointment and start to think about the evening being ruined now. It's not going the way I planned. At the same time I start to feel guilty and selfish for feeling that way. I'm completely stuck. I can usually catch myself now, but sometimes this way of thinking goes on for a while, taking me out of the present moment and ruining the moments that haven't even happened yet. I might share with Matthew my experience of disappointment, and he might apologize for including others without checking with me. But really it isn't just about that. It's more about my letting go and not being attached to my expectation for the event. Most times I enjoy the company, and an added benefit is that I'm awed by Matthews's generosity and kindness in being so big-hearted with his spontaneous invitations. I get more present to his big, all inclusive heart, which I love about him.

If I'm giving, living and loving 100%, playing full out, surrendering to the opportunity to love and be loved, and then letting go, any attachment would inhibit what I'm actually creating. I can see that no one walks out of a great relationship. Attachment stifles, restricts, and limits what is possible. I can also see that it is often based in my own insecurity. If I'm all in, then if for some reason my relationship ended as I knew it, I would have no regrets. I played full out. But if I don't give it all I have, or hold on and keep it safe and it ends as I know it, then I may say to myself, "I should have been more... I wish I had... If only...." In other words, I will have some experience of regret.

I am considering that everything that anyone says is either a request for love, "Love me!," or an expression of it, "I love you." I'm starting to listen for the request for love, or the expression of love, in all conversations. What would be my response to the request, "Love me"? What would be my response to "I love you"? I can see that to either it is the same: love.

Practice:
I know I'm perfect Spirit, I know I'm Divine, I know I am whole and complete unto myself so I choose to be love and give, give, give....

When god sends rain, rain is my choice.
—Werner Erhard

I Am Choosing
Can I choose to love it all just the way it is?

Ultimately my mastery, my fulfillment and my relationships come down to my choosing, not resisting what is present in this moment. Can I choose what I choose, what I give my word to, day after day after day? Can I choose breaking my word? Can I choose wants and desires, my egoic machinery, and let it do my choosing? Can I choose the wounds and nastiness of others? Can I choose my judgments, opinions, shame and inadequacy? What happens when I stop resisting my human predicament, the stormy weather of separation, and just choose to experience my experience?

What happens when I am being, "This is it"? I choose "This, right now." My partner, this job, this body, this thought – choose. My mother – choose. Bankruptcy – choose. Prison – choose. When I resist my life, I'm stuck. When I choose my life, anything is possible. We don't choose life for just any reason; we choose to live at choice. Choosing creates aliveness and vitality; resistance creates lethargy. *Your duty is to choose, not to choose this or that. (Zen Koan)*

God is handling my awakening. I choose all my life circumstances like a warrior whose life depends on it. Circumstances are all there for me to forgive, release, and lean into, as aids to my liberation. I choose all my relations. They are my teachers of unconditional love. I am inspired by Nelson Mandela who chose to teach his captors how to read and chose to emerge from prison after twenty-six years a gracious human being.

I choose to not judge myself for judging, or when I am small and petty. Choosing to choose me, others and all of life

74.

reaches my ecstatic majesty. In choosing, I exercise my Christhood.

Unless I choose to love someone, they won't fully reveal themselves to me. Why should they? They aren't safe from my judgment until I love them unconditionally. When I choose to love, I grant being to however people show up in my life. By loving them, they are safe to choose love as well. This is the cornerstone of a functional human community. It starts with me. The Second Coming is being birthed in my heart. Everyday is an exercise in choosing love.

Paddy's story

I have been developing a close relationship with Mielle for seven years. We have been through all sorts of spaces in our relationship. We have become very close friends, co-workers, housemates, and in the next few days, we are becoming co-parents of a new baby.

I remember when she told me she was pregnant almost nine and a half months ago, I said, "I am willing to raise this child." I didn't really think about it; it was just there for me to say. I just knew that I would do anything for this baby. The father was not going to be raising the child, and Mielle really wanted the baby to be supported by her community. We both thought about it more and talked it over, and then one day simply chose to be co-parents. She is due to give birth any day now, and I am legally adopting the baby as the second parent.

We chose a very non-traditional route, and I can see why this path is not a common one. So many things have challenged me. Some days I feel like our choice threatens all my previous visions for my life, even the most common one: fall in love with a man, get married, raise babies together and live happily ever after. Our choice has certainly challenged my parents' vision for my life.

There are also many miracles I can be *present* to. At the baby shower which our community hosted for us, my mother came and experienced all the love of our friends and how special this child is to all of us. It might have been easy to let our minds diminish her presence, creating that she really "had" to be there, but then we read the card that came with her gift and got teary-eyed when we saw it was addressed to both Mielle and me. We felt so accepted and acknowledged.

Most of the time I relish the path we have chosen. I also see that having chosen to be a parent of this child does not necessarily have to interfere with any and all other possibilities for my life. I can create any possible future. This child, this choice, is an addition to the large circle of love in which we already reside. We're asked to stretch ourselves in order to include all possibilities. I am often encouraged by remembering that choosing is simply empowering whatever choice I make. This is real freedom.

Practice:
I ask myself all day long, "What would love do now?"
(As if love were an entity or your identity.)

each
other

as
guru

Unless I love something completely
it will not reveal itself to me.
—Rudolph Steiner

INTIMATE PARTNERSHIP
"What can you reveal to your partner
that you are afraid to reveal?"

Intimate partnership is an invented context for relationship, an exercise in the non-stop surrender of a completely merged life. It's a fellowship of effort and transcendence. Living from the "we" is a practice in mindfulness – consciously choosing Oneness-thinking, speaking, believing, acting and attitudes of Oneness. I am asking myself this: "Am I up for inviting a 24/7 mirror and an emotional monitor into my life? Am I consenting to make being present the purpose of my life and use the degree of love present in the relationship as a gauge of my success? Am I willing to make my life about our joint awakening? Am I willing to forsake the miserable comfort of separateness for the unrelenting reminder to let go?"

MATTHEW'S VOWS

Terces, I am that your life and our life is Great.

I am that our children's lives are great.

I promise to create and behold you as my passionate
lover, my Kindred Spirit, an honor to have in my life.

I promise to be worthy of the blessing you are to me.

I promise to love the man you love and
to stand for you loving the woman I love.

Terces, how you will know me is great-full.

You will know the difference you make
as my beloved.

Terces, I promise that generosity is the star
by which I navigate.

Terces, I am your worshipper until I have to let go.

I devote myself to you in the readiness for devotion at
a Divine level.

We are one life.

TERCES' VOWS

I, Terces, promise you, Matthew, to be the gracious and loving wife of a most extraordinary man. To awaken each day loving you completely and to snuggle together at night knowing we have fulfilled on Being Love for one another and for everyone else. I promise to always listen to you and be moved by the powerful and Sacred expression of Spirit you are.

I promise to be the woman behind the man making a difference in the world that enriches your soul, and has you being the champion for yourself and others that inspire you.

I promise to laugh with you, to cry with you, and to be still and passionate with you. I promise to love our children as the precious human beings they are and to be a woman they can count on for wisdom and love. I promise to be that giving and receiving are one and the same and to be an opening for the unceasing flow of everything.

You will know me as being grateful for all the miracles of life, and for the difference you make as the love of my life.

I promise to moment by moment create our partnership as an endless discovery of what's possible and to be that no matter what we might be facing our world is always being given by The Divine.

I promise to love the woman you love and to always stand for you loving the man I love. I promise to never forget the day I discovered I love you like I love Jesus.

I am your devoted woman; we are one life.

My life far surpassed my expectations long ago. We own two organic farms and a transformational business that makes a difference; we've authored several books; we lead workshops, travel extensively and have five amazing children and four grandchildren. All of this is wonderful, and the greatest wonder in my life is not a thing; it's my relationship with Terces. We joke about being the motivational speakers that "live in a van down by the river," but many days living that simply, having lots of quality time for each other, sounds really yummy. The space that Terces holds for me extracts me from my head and moves me to my heart. I had a teacher who said, "Without my partner I'm just a nice tan looking for an orgasm."

Intimate partnership is creating each other as the guru. In intimate partnership the other is either demonstrating love or calling me to be more loving. Terces sees and relates to my Divine nature even when I can't, even when I'm being a jerk. We are each other's Zen masters, training one another in non attachment – giving, living, and loving 100%, with no expectations. We create this by conversing with and acknowledging each other's love presence, even when one or both of our egos is activated. Our job is to hold space for each other without coaching, fixing or pointing out when we think the other is being run by their wounds. We recreate one another and let the weather pass. With understanding of the charm of form and how insidious fear is, we each give our oath to the seat of love, allowing Oneness to fill the space. When we forget to hold space for each other we apologize and recommit.

A therapist once told me, "if you want to check in on your spiritual progress, examine your relationship with money, family, and intimate partnership."

I am getting present to the belief that nowhere is my shadow (hungry ghost) more activated than around money and intimate partnership.

Money is never the problem, only my misplaced perception of it. Money brings up all my security issues because my ego is always threatened and thinks security lies in the outer. Death is ego's central myth, its fear of being extinguished, the source of scarcity. Intimate partnership is the possibility of putting all my security issues on the table, holding space for each other's experience and consciously choosing being trustful. I say, "If our money is not together, then we are not fully together." If money and what it represents, security in the outer, is valued, given priority over One-ness and trust, then our relationship still has a ways to go in order to grow. If my partner is threatened by sharing funds, there is more love for us to recover. I am not saying this is the truth, or that it's bad. I can see it is okay to choose having separate money in a re-lationship, but I am considering that if it is costing me relatedness with my partner and ultimately my Higher Self, I am still invested in separateness.

We coach many couples, and money often comes up as an issue cloaking the ego's unwillingness to let go. In our relationship I was the one inheriting money. I was now going to have more, and that was just as much of a stretch for me: receiving more, being responsible for more, and trusting more. My life had been designed around what I had. Having more redesigned my life, and as a result, I had to let go of my resistance to having more. Some people think having more is easy. I promise you it has just as many challenges as having less. It isn't about quantity, it is about who am I being. I am not more grateful now; I am simply grateful now.

I am considering that we really aren't all that complicated. Consider that we only have two modalities: fear and doubt, or love and trust. Which one do I want to partner with? What kind of part-ner do I want to be in return? The only reason I'm afraid to let go, to give fully of myself and my resources is because I fear it won't be reciprocated. It may not, not in the way I might think, but who cares? I give in order to release my perception of scarcity (lack of love, money, etc.). The Gospel says, "turn the other cheek," be-cause love can't be threatened. For me, leadership signifies going first and being fully committed. Playing small I cannot reach my

majesty.

Transparency demonstrates the value of giving up our defenses. In intimate partnership I recommend full disclosure. I let my partner into the full nasty selfishness of my false identity; it's a role I sometimes forget I'm playing. Together we can laugh at the severed heads and lame costumes of the grade B horror movie that is our smallness. We can play a game of one-upping each other by sharing our own personal monsters.

Early on in my relationship with Terces she asked me to share something that I didn't want to share. She is the space of acceptance. I felt completely safe to reveal that I desired most women and that I thought about having sex with many of the women I encountered. This admission was a relief. I no longer had to hide the sexual machinery that was running me. We could go to a restaurant and I'd point out her, and her, and her, not her, and her. I was free. No more concealing my sexuality out of shame. I now have the machinery, but the machinery doesn't have me. Terces entered the world of the testosterone mechanism and felt compassion and understanding for the male predicament – screw it or kill it. For a survivor of sexual abuse this was a true healing. Just like I joke about the pranks of the ego, Terces and I get to laugh at the antics of the male engine – it doesn't mean anything. It isn't personal; it's a zillion year old survival mechanism that is etched in our genes.

I have learned for myself and most women, feeling beautiful is a tall order. It can also be a trap. I can rationalize that I don't want to fall into the beautiful-or-not paradigm. But how do I separate myself from it when it seems to be all around me? I remember sitting on the edge of my mother's bed during the last few weeks of her life. She was bedridden and needed to be turned and cared for on an hourly basis, and still her conversation included observations about her body, "Oh my hands are so thin," and, "I have lost so much muscle my skin just hangs on me. I'm glad your Daddy never had to see me like this."

And how about this one: "I hardly eat and still I bet I haven't lost any weight!"

Does it never end? I wondered. While I know that beauty is inside and I can feel it most when I have my attention on serving others rather than on myself, I wish for all of us the end of this anxiety. I am inspired by the healthy young beautiful women I work with, and yet I hear them questioning their beauty and diminishing their worth. I ached for Matthew when I realized what it must be like for a man to be haunted by a never-ending sexual urge. I could see the impact that particular hungry ghost has had on my own feminine experience. How do I love myself just the way I am, when my machinery is all about attracting a man and keeping his attention? I have taken on and invite you to practice sitting down, being still and confident in your own inner beauty, that beauty which never fades, nor can it be diminished by time or circumstance.

Practices

1. We are not each other's coaches.
We find a coach if we want one.

2. If our money's not together, we are not together.

3. We schedule dates, quality time, sex.
We create themes, dates, fantasies, etc.

4. We recreate and clear each other continuously.

5. We use all the Kindred Spiritisms and tools
(see pages 93 & 102).

6. If I am thinking about breaking up, I give our relationship six months and play full out at being unconditional love, and after that I choose to recreate our relationship, or not.

7. If we do choose to move out of intimate partnership with one another, we leave each other in great shape, acknowledge the contribution we were to each other's lives. We create a new context for our relationship that inspires us.

8. We play the "Share What You Don't Want to Share" game often.

9. My job is not to fix, change, or point out my partner's baggage or wounds. I simply hold space and recreate them. I know my partner is training me in Christ consciousness.

10. Rather ~~then~~ than snap at each other, we agree to "growl." Growling or howling at life (into space) when emotional energy (frustration, anger, etc.) is moving through helps to dissipate the energy rather then direct it at each other.

As a single footstep will not make a path on the earth, so a single thought will not make a pathway in the mind. To make a deep physical path, we walk again and again. To make a mental path, we must think over and over the kind of thoughts we wish to dominate our lives.
—Henry David Thoreau

TOOLS OF THE TRADE
"With whom am I unwilling to practice love"

What I have in my life, be it love, wealth, family, health, I have because I've given my word to it, committed to it and taken the actions consistent to that commitment: I've practiced being healthy, wealthy and wise. What I don't have in my life I haven't given my word to. I haven't given my word to playing a musical instrument, being a surfer, or being organized. This is no big mystery. I know it takes practice and discipline to achieve flexibility and yet I resist going to yoga, even though after a yoga session I feel so recharged.

Part of my ego machinery resists domination by any structure. I may find myself resisting even the structure of these practices. Yet I ask myself how dominating is it to have the relationships in my life not work? The only formal training I have received in relationship and managing my emotions is from my parents. Creating awakened *relationship* takes practice. Living free from the constraints of the ego takes mindfulness. I have two choices. I can choose to create my life from loving moment to loving moment

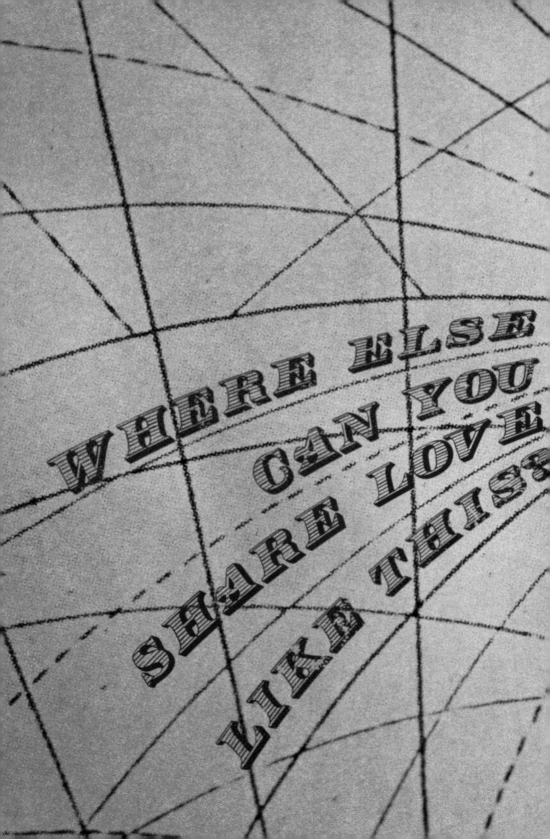

or endure an existence of the habitual reruns of my ego's terror. Establishing the sacred container of relationship is an ongoing ceremony, a daily devotion in being occupied by a Supreme Love Presence. Here are my tools of the trade.

Tools

1. Upsets are not personal; they are not responding to me.

2. My acknowledgments evoke the Divine presence.

3. I make powerful requests as an exercise in worthiness and remember that "no" doesn't mean anything. I build my self-worth by making powerful requests, and I get at least one "no" everyday.

4. I give the people in my life what I want to receive.

5. I recreate everyone. When I recreate, I insure that the people in my life are heard and that I am in their world.

6. I apologize first and all the time. I take 100% responsibility.

7. I am more committed to being kind than being right.

8. I don't gossip or listen to gossip. I don't tolerate any speaking that diminishes another human being. (I make requests rather than gossip.)

9. I often ask myself, "What would love do now?"

10. I practice forgiveness. I grant everyone their own awakening process. All "sins" (actions that miss the mark of love) are equally meaningless.

11. I practice non-attachment. Giving, living and loving 100%, with no expectations.

12. To everyone in my life – my employees, boss, spouse, broth-

ers, sisters, friends – I check in and say, "My job is that you have a great life. How is your life? How am I doing?" I ask, "Do you have any requests of me?" (See example #4.)

13. I ask, "What did you hear me say?" as a way to mirror and diffuse the energy of someone reacting to a neutral statement I have made. (See example #1.)

14. I say, "You're not wanting me to feel something other than love, are you?" as a mirror and diffuser of perceived criticism coming at me. (See example #2.)

15. I ask, "What do you need to hear from me to restore love to our relationship?" This is my courageous act of transparency and a powerful request of responsibility. (See example #3.)

16. I ask, "Where else are we going to share love like this?" This query is actually a declaration in the form of a question, which locates me, the speaker, inside a commitment of the now moment: this is it, we are it, you are it, now. (See example #3.)

17. I say, "I am making up that _____." This is a tool I use that gives me 100% responsibility for my position or story. It is a way I open the space in a relationship that has become stuck. (See example #4.)

18. I say, "I need your help. I just need you to hear me. You don't need to do anything with what I say. I'm just sharing my experience." This is an opening I apply when communicating something difficult, uncomfortable or challenging, while setting up my listener powerfully. (See example #4.)

19. "I am love listening to that thought." I use this mantra to stay centered in love when I perceive someone is upset with me or critical of me. In this context, with regard to what they are saying, I inwardly say to myself, "I am love listening to that thought; I am love listening to that thought."

Here are some examples of restoring love on the court, in your life.

Example #1

Kindred Spirit A
"Would you please wash the dishes?"

Kindred Spirit B
"You're always nagging me." (upset)

Kindred Spirit A
"What did you hear me say?" (tool #13)

Kindred Spirit B
"I heard you say, 'Would you please wash the dishes?'"

Kindred Spirit A
"Great! That is what I said."

OR

Kindred Spirit B
"I heard you say, 'You never do enough around here.'"

Kindred Spirit A
"I apologize if I spoke in any way to diminish you. I really only meant to say, 'Would you please wash the dishes?'"
(Apology tool #6)

OR

Kindred Spirit A
"You're right, I thought you weren't doing your fair share, and I apologize for not being honest with you." (Apology tool #6)

Example #2

Kindred Spirit A
"You thought Africa was a country?" (put down)

Kindred Spirit B
"You don't want me to feel something other than love, do you?"
(tool # 14)

Kindred Spirit A
"No, I don't. I apologize for my conceit. I got too big for my britches. If you have any geography questions, just ask me."
(Apology tool #6)

Example #3

Kindred Spirit A
"Where have you been?" (upset)

Kindred Spirit B
"I was at the park and ran into friends."

Kindred Spirit A
"You always have time for everyone else but me." (upset)

Kindred Spirit B
"So what I hear you say is that you were wondering where I was and that you think I always have time for everyone else but you."
(Recreation tool # 5)

Kindred Spirit A
"Yes, and I feel abandoned and angry."

Kindred Spirit B
"And you feel abandoned and angry."   (Recreation tool #5)

Kindred Spirit A
"Yes."

Kindred Spirit B
"I apologize for not calling, for being oblivious to the time, for leaving you with the experience that I don't have time for you. Do you accept my apology?" (Apology tool #6)

Kindred Spirit A
"Yes."

Kindred Spirit B
"What do you need to hear from me to restore love to our relationship?"   (tool # 15)

Kindred Spirit A
"My request is that you say that you understand that I want to spend time with you, and I request that you to make the same request of me." (Request tool #3)

Kindred Spirit B
"Baby, I so understand how much you want to spend time with me, and I love spending time with you. I am all in. My request is that you gently remind me when you have the experience that I am not being attentive. Commitment is new for me." (Request tool #3)

Kindred Spirit A
"I accept your request. I apologize for being grouchy. I traveled down my abandonment tunnel." (Apology tool #6)

Kindred Spirit B
"Thank you for training me in being attentive. Thank you for being patient with me." (Acknowledgment tool #2) "And babe, where else are we going to share love like this? (tool #16)

Kindred Spirit A
"You're the best. I love you." (Acknowledgment tool #2)

Example # 4

Kindred Spirit A
"I have a request that you hear me out. You don't have to do anything with what I say. Just listen. This is my experience, okay?" (Request tool #3 and tool #18)

Kindred Spirit B
"Okay."

Kindred Spirit A
"I'm making up that you are not inspired by your work anymore, you're bored and you're going to quit soon." (tool #17)

Kindred Spirit B
"Wow, that's quite a story. I actually have no plans to quit. Work is actually my salvation these days. If my performance is off it's what is going on at home that is distracting me. My wife and I are going through a divorce and it's rough on the kids; I feel devastated. "

Kindred Spirit A
"I'm really sorry to hear that. I apologize for not checking in sooner. I also apologize for making all that up about you." (Apology tool #6)

Kindred Spirit B
"Thanks."

Kindred Spirit A
"As your boss, my job is that your life works. Do you have any requests of me?"   (tool #12)

Kindred Spirit B
"I request that you check in with me once a week, if that's okay." (Request tool #3)

Kindred Spirit A
"I accept your request. I'd like to acknowledge you for your courage and transparency."   (Acknowledgment tool #2)

Kindred Spiritisms

I make it all up.

When I am listening I am being the highest form of loving.

If I want comfort I'll get a pet dog.

I love to lean into the discomfort.

I know my feelings and everyone's emotional experiences are transient – akin to weather that's just passing through our lives.

Emotional experiences I don't enjoy are revealing to me my separation thinking.

I know that nothing is wrong.

Being right is costing me my aliveness.

I know "no" doesn't mean anything. I love making requests, and I am not stopped by "no."

Nothing real can be threatened,
nothing unreal exists.
—A Course in Miracles

ALL MY RELATIONS!
"Whom am I unwilling to forgive?"

J sit in a paradox. In one hand I hold what I am calling a more
indigenous view of life. This view honors the great mother earth on
which I sit and discerns my responsibility to harmonize all my relations so that this earth school might continue its precious purpose.
In the other hand I hold a view that the charm or apparent realness
of this world of form is my real challenge, and to forgive myself
and all sentient beings for becoming absorbed by the *material* is
my purpose, for through that forgiveness, it shall disappear. Perhaps there is no paradox here, but there are days when I diminish
myself for being attached to materiality, expressed as my obsession
with organic farming and sustainability. "I should be more spiritual," my ego asserts. And I am clear that if I made my life about being in ceremony and non-stop Vipassana meditation, I'd be dealing
with another of ego's judgments, "I should be living a life of more
service."

   With my hands in the soil I feel connected to my roots and
synchronized with the rhythms of the earth. Yet so much of what is
my calling finds me on the paved asphalt of the big city. I consider
that it doesn't matter where I am, can I bring the balance to my life
that inspires me to walk the spiritual path with practical feet? Can I
simply be happy wherever and with whomever? Can I open up and
let love shine through me no matter what?

Ego's allegiance is solely to its own survival; its bloated self-importance ensures both the demise of mother earth and the delay of our ascendance. No matter what spiritual context I'm holding, the ego's grip obstructs my vision and fulfillment. Both the outer life (war, environmental, social, and political degradation) and the inner (unrest, pharmaceutical use, rampant addiction, intolerance and fundamentalism), are screaming for revolutionary overthrow. The dethroning of that of which I speak is the crowning triumph of love over fear and eternal life over bodily death. It consists in forgiving all of our relations and ourselves for all the ways we've forged our aloneness real and certified its authenticity. *Kindred Spirit* is a way to be an ongoing activist in the cause of Eternal Love. As courageous as standing before an army tank, being a *Kindred Spirit* requires giving up on an evidence-based consensus reality and relentlessly giving our obeisance to the consciousness of love.

The occurring is that ego is winning most of the battles, but that is a time-based news report from the impostor itself. Can a flea usurp a lion? Can a candle outshine the sun? There never was a war, only Divine patience inviting us to let go of what never could be. There is nothing easy about this passage, and I don't expect crowds to cheer me on. I assert that this is the work of our generation, to forgive all atrocities as cast from the same lie, while fulfilling love's promise, to cause a Kindred Community of all humankind. We are it!

Can a flea usurp a lion?

Can a candle outshine the sun?

There was never a war at all.

ABOUT THE AUTHORS

$\mathcal{M}$atthew and Terces are the loves of each other's lives. Together they practice being a source of unconditional love. Their inspiring relationship has caused a community to gather around them: Café Gratitude, Gracias Madre, Be Love Farm, Laulima Farm in Maui, Café Gratitude Los Angeles, and Gratitude communities in Kansas City and Mexico.

Matthew and Terces live together on Be Love Farm in Vacaville, California. They live in community on 21 acres, practicing a sustainable lifestyle and regenerative agriculture. Matthew and Terces offer monthly workshops on Sacred Commerce, the Being of Abundance, and Relationship as a Path of Awakening.

For more information please visit **www.cafegratitude.com**.

The Engelharts have previously published five books and a board game: *The Abounding River Personal Logbook, I Am Grateful: Recipes and Lifestyle of Café Gratitude, Sweet Gratitude: A New World of Raw Desserts, Sacred Commerce: Business as a Path of Awakening, Plenty of Time: A 366 Day Creative Planner* and *The Abounding River Board Game*.

THANK YOU FOR **FULFILLING LOVE'S PROMISE**
WITH US.
Love, *Matthew and Terces*